Chronology of Public Health
in the United States

Chronology of Public Health in the United States

RUSSELL O. WRIGHT

McFarland & Company, Inc., Publishers
Jefferson, North Carolina, and London

LIBRARY OF CONGRESS CATALOGUING-IN-PUBLICATION DATA

Wright, Russell O.
    Chronology of public health in the United States /
Russell O. Wright.
        p.   cm.
    Includes bibliographical references and index.

    ISBN 0-7864-2194-0 (softcover : 50# alkaline paper)

    1. Public Health — United States — History. I. Title.
[DNLM: 1. Public Health — history — United States —
chronology. WA 11 AA1 W952c 2005]
    RA445.W75   2005
    362.1'0973 — dc22   2005001731

British Library cataloguing data are available

Cover photograph ©2005 Brand X Pictures

Manufactured in the United States of America

McFarland & Company, Inc., Publishers
   Box 611, Jefferson, North Carolina 28640
   www.mcfarlandpub.com

To Eleanor Fern Wright Graul

CONTENTS

ACKNOWLEDGMENTS

As I have done in the prior books in this series, I want to acknowledge the active participation of my wife, Halina Wright, and my daughter, Terry Ann Wright, in the completion of this latest book in the informally linked Chronology series I have been doing (see page ii). Halina continued to collect appropriate research material from the Internet, our local libraries, and the *Los Angeles Times*. She also served as editor for the final manuscript.

Terry continued to use her mastery of Microsoft Word to create the final typed manuscript, including the figures in the appendix. Her equally great mastery of the Internet produced much research material, and her handprint, in one of these respects, is on every page of this book.

Once again, it is the Wright Writing Enterprise that continues to produce these chronologies.

INTRODUCTION

A chronology of public health is closely related to the chronology of the broader subject of medicine and its struggle against human disease. The strongest challengers on earth to humans, besides other humans, are the microscopic life forms of bacteria and viruses (viruses are arguably not a true life form). The battle between the human race and its microscopic opponents has being going on since humans first arrived on earth. There is a complex array of people engaged in this battle. The first line is composed of doctors, who carry out their tasks within a large number of specialties. Doctors also try to defeat — or at least delay the terminal effects of— a number of chronic illnesses that eventually affect the human race even if the attacks of our microscopic invaders are avoided or successfully defeated.

Doctors in most specialties do their primary work either in the treatment of individual patients who come to them or in the research laboratory. Doctors and related support personnel working in the specialty of public health concentrate on bringing to the public the weapons created by medicine in the fight against infectious disease or chronic illness. Public health specialists do this via programs to immunize masses of people against infectious diseases and by educating people about health practices and lifestyle choices most likely to avoid infectious disease and chronic illness. The division of labor between medicine as a whole and public health practitioners is reasonably clear today, but the present arrangement took a long time to develop.

This chronology is a record of that development. Accordingly, this introduction is meant to establish a basic understanding of the infectious and chronic diseases that medicine is trying to overcome. This permits the best understanding of the roles doctors focusing on individuals and those focusing on public health must play. Also, this introduction will show how the internal defenses of humans are organized to fight disease processes so that the attempts of medicine to support those defenses also can be best understood.

The Threat of Infectious Disease

Since life has existed on earth, it has taken a wide range of forms, including some that seem beyond our imagination. These forms have ranged in size from microscopic viruses that can only be seen using electron microscopes with powers of magnification on the order of one million to creatures like the great blue whale that weighs over one hundred tons. The only constant is that each form of life sees other forms as a source of food and nourishment and conducts its life cycle accordingly.

Some scientists have said that life on earth exists at the bottom of an ocean of air we call the atmosphere. Human beings have learned to rule the visible creatures in this ocean by using tools and weapons reflecting the highly developed mental capabilities of the human race. But the prime competition for surviving in this ocean is the life forms that cannot be seen with the unaided human eye. The world in which we live is literally alive with various bacteria and viruses, and they live all over and within our bodies as well. These tiny bacterial and viral life forms are often known as microparasites. They find a home for survival in human, animal, or plant hosts. Some contribute to the survival of their host and stay with the host indefinitely. Others cause deleterious effects that we call disease and can be lethal to the host.

The bacteria included in these life forms may represent the oldest form of life on earth. Bacteria are similar in many ways to the trillions of cells in our bodies. Bacteria eat and dispose of wastes and reproduce by cell division. In these ways they are clearly alive. However, a virus lives on the edge of life and non-life. It is a thousand times smaller than a bacterium or human cell. Some scientists call them nothing more than a tiny hypodermic needle packed with DNA or RNA. Viruses are relatively small because they contain none of the basic processes for life as we know it. They invade cells and take over the elaborate structures in the cell by injecting their piece of DNA or RNA into the cell and reproducing themselves using the elegant mechanisms of the cell. This is the only way viruses can reproduce. Once they have replicated within the cell hundreds of times, they destroy the cell and break out into the bloodstream looking for new cells to victimize. Accordingly, the virus can easily produce a disease that is often fatal. Other times they are "at peace" within one kind of host and are fatal to other kinds of hosts. Notably, viruses produce respiratory diseases that compromise the ability of humans to extract and process oxygen from the ocean of air they live in, thus leading to terminal results. The original word "virus" comes from the Latin for "poison," which is certainly appropriate in terms of viral effects on humans and animals. It is also appropriate for the additional modern meaning of attacks by a virus on computers.

In the medical sense, viruses also invade a number of plants including wheat, maize (corn), sugar cane, soybeans, and potatoes, thus affecting the human food supply. In humans, viruses produce such diseases as the common cold, influenza, measles, mumps, yellow fever, chicken pox, smallpox, polio, rabies, and AIDS, to name only a few. Viruses are also now known to cause some kinds of cancer in animals and humans. Bacteria produce such diseases as tuberculosis, typhoid, leprosy, cholera, diphtheria, tetanus, pneumonia, plague, botulism, and dysentery, and many other diseases. A key difference between diseases caused by viruses and bacteria is that agents called antibiotics can kill bacteria because they have a structure and life cycle similar to that of our own cells. Thus, that life cycle can be interfered with to the extent that the bacteria, or its ability to reproduce itself, are destroyed.

Viruses have no such structure, and thus can be killed in the body only by the immune system that seeks them out and destroys them. But if the immune system takes too long to respond, the virus will kill the person first. Therefore, the best defense for a virus is what we call vaccination, which prepares the immune system to be ready to fight a viral infection with sufficient speed to conquer the virus before it kills the person. The same basic concept applies to bacteria. It is always better to prevent a disease than to try to cure it after the fact, even if antibiotics are available to help fight the bacteria.

An Immune System Primer

The prime parts of the body involved in the immune system are the bone marrow, the thymus, the spleen, and the lymph nodes. They produce or nurture cells whose job is to seek out invaders in the body and destroy them. Many special cells are part of this process, but one major cell type is the B lymphocytes, or simply the B cells. These cells carry molecules on the surface called antibodies. These antibodies can stick to other molecules and come in such a variety of shapes that at least one usually will stick to any new invading microbe (the molecule to which an antibody sticks is called an antigen). Once an antigen is found, the B cell with the proper antibody begins to divide rapidly to create more antibodies. The invader cell has essentially been marked for death, but it takes about two weeks to generate enough new B cells to mark a substantial quantity of the invaders. Once they are marked, large white blood cells called phagocytes arrive to eat the marked invaders.

This process is greatly speeded up if the invader appears for a second time and is recognized when encountered again. Cells called memory B cells remaining from the first attack go into action immediately and enable the immune system to respond in two or three days rather than two weeks. The invader is wiped out before it can reproduce to the degree needed to seriously affect us. We may not even notice it was there the second time. The presence of these memory cells means we are immune to future attacks by that invader. This immunity can remain for a number of years or even a lifetime.

In the case of a virus, the same process applies, but the B cells can only mark those viruses found traveling freely in the bloodstream. The huge number of viruses hiding within our cells cannot be marked. In this case, the immune system turns to T cells. These T cells can sense when a virus is inside one of our cells based on the condition of the surface of the invaded cell. When an infected cell is found, the T cell calls in specialized killer cells to destroy it. Finally, the phagocyte white cells come in to clean up the remains of the battle. Again, if the invader is successfully defeated, memory T cells remain in the system to give the survivor immunity, as was the case with the B cells after an attack by a bacterium. These killer T cells also act against the tumor cells of cancer, but the process is even more complicated than the battle against regular infectious disease.

The immune system is much more complex than described here, but the basic facts show why vaccination is so important. Vaccination (and its predecessor, called inoculation) introduces the immune system to deadly bacterial or viral life forms in a way that does not harm the person to be treated. Antibodies against the diseases are created as well as the proper memory cells. When the disease attempts to attack naturally, the immune system sees it as the second attack and is ready to rapidly defend us. We will have much more to say about inoculation and vaccination, and the difference between the two, but for now it is only necessary to understand how these processes help to defend us by giving us immunity. It was the lack of immunity to European diseases that killed millions of Native Americans when the Spanish in the early 1500s brought smallpox to people that had no immunity to it. A basic understanding of the immune system and the way it works is necessary to be able to understand the threat of AIDS and other new diseases in our rapidly shrinking world.

Infectious Diseases and the Response of Public Health

Today, public health doctors and officials basically bring the advances of medicine to the entire population via vaccination and educational programs. But when the entire field of medicine is "blind," as it was until about the 1880s with respect to infectious disease, there are precious few advances to bring to the population. However, even when the causes of disease are not known, simply observing the process of a disease, including who gets sick and who doesn't, can lead to cures and treatments that produce results in spite of the fact that no one knows exactly why. Probably the best example of this is smallpox.

Smallpox is an ancient disease that has plagued the human race for many centuries. Many people do not know that smallpox was given that name to differentiate it from the "great pox" of syphilis, another ancient disease. Smallpox was such a killer that even aside from the ravages it caused among the Indian tribes beginning in the 1500s, there was a saying in relatively advanced England that no one should count the number of children they have had until after each child had survived "the smallpox." And even though this chronology is specifically about public health in the United States, many events took place outside the United States before 1900 that determined the course of public health in the United States. So we must include these events in the chronology, wherever they took place.

One of the first attempts to avoid smallpox was made around 950 (A.D.) in China. It had been observed there, as elsewhere, that any survivor of the disease never got it again, no matter how many times the disease reappeared in epidemics. Whether the person only got a few of the ugly pus-filled scabs that marked the disease or was covered with them, as long as they survived they never got the disease again. Someone made the connection that even a mild case of the disease produced immunity (they did not use that word per se). Not knowing the mechanism that produced that immunity but grasping its importance, people took scabs from a recovering patient, ground them into a powder, and in a process called insufflation, the powder was blown up the nose of a person to be protected.

The technique seemed to work. The new patient got (generally) a mild attack of smallpox but then easily recovered and was immune from that time on. Today we know that the donor, on the road to recovery, had already conquered the smallpox virus. What was blown up the next person's nose was a weakened or even killed form of the virus. Antibodies and memory cells were produced accordingly even if the basic virus was weakened or even killed, and the new patient was immune in the sense that any new attack by the smallpox virus would produce only mild symptoms, if any at all.

Smallpox takes about 12 days to get established, with the variola virus that causes smallpox beginning to reproduce itself millions of times by then. Thus, the natural immune system response of two weeks is often too late to avoid being overwhelmed by the disease. An immune person generates enough antibodies in just two or three days, and thus it is the disease that is overwhelmed in the case of an immune response. If people were not immune, the disease killed about one-third of its victims and caused such defects as blindness in many others. In the case of the Indians killed by the arrival of the Europeans, whole communities perished because many survivors of the disease died of other causes when not enough people were left to feed and take care of them.

The terrible consequences of smallpox meant that traders were anxious to spread the apparent Chinese "cure" quickly across Asia and west as far as Turkey by the late 1600s. By then the practice had changed to the extent that the people to be protected were cut on the arm and pus taken from a recovering victim was introduced into the scratch. This process came to be called inoculation from a Greek word for the grafting of buds from a healthy plant on another plant to improve the condition of a second plant.

A report on this process made its way to the Royal Society of London in 1713. Soon after, Lady Mary Worthley Montagu, the wife of the British ambassador to Turkey, who had had smallpox in her younger years (leaving her with facial scars and no eyebrows) and had lost a brother to the disease, became involved in the practice of inoculation. Her six-year-old son was inoculated in Turkey in 1717, and after returning to London in 1720, her three-year-old daughter was inoculated as a new wave of smallpox hit the city. Both children were unaffected by the new outbreak of smallpox. After newspapers picked up the story, Lady Mary Montagu became a vocal proponent of inoculation, and soon Princess Caroline, wife of the next king, George II, became interested in trying it to protect her young daughters.

After a series of "volunteers" were inoculated in the summer of 1721 without ill effect (the "volunteers" included persons in prison who had been sentenced to death but escaped hanging by agreeing to be inoculated, as well as children in orphanages), the royal children were inoculated successfully. Inoculation became a small industry in England and parts of Europe, with doctors charging high fees to those, usually the wealthy, who could pay.

But inoculation had its dangers. People being inoculated were being given smallpox after all, and in some cases they got a still-virulent case of the disease and died. Data show that about 1 in 50 persons in England died from inoculation in the decade after 1721. Because inoculated patients had a real case of smallpox (hopefully mild), they could spread the disease to those not inoculated. Thus, they had to be isolated until their self-imposed disease had run its course. All but the wealthy went to primitive inoculation stables, which were appropriately named. Because no one knew yet how or why the process worked, patients were subjected to bleeding and fed medicines to cleanse their bodies. These medicines had no effect on the process except to make it almost a form of torture.

This changed when Edward Jenner developed a true vaccination process in 1796. Jenner had undergone the inoculation process himself when he was a young boy and remembered the process with horror. He was born in 1749 into a family of nine children headed by a country minister of the church, but both his father and mother died within weeks of each other when Jenner was five. He was raised by an older brother who took over both the family and the church, and who managed to get Jenner a place in the inoculation process when Jenner was eight years old (not everyone could afford it). Jenner's older brother later arranged for Jenner to be apprenticed to a surgeon in 1763 when he was 14.

A surgeon in those days was a relatively lowly profession. They lanced boils, set broken bones, stitched up cuts, pulled teeth, and when necessary amputated infected fingers, arms, and legs to prevent blood poisoning. Jenner was successful in this profession and set up a practice in the country town of Berkeley in western England where he was born, even though he was invited to stay in London after being an apprentice there. Jenner much preferred the country. In 1792 he received the official title of doctor through a process that required the payment of cash and some letters of recommendation.

By then, at the age of 43, Jenner had been looking for a better way to prevent smallpox than inoculation, even though he gave inoculations himself, as did other doctors. In his country practice he had long recognized the fact that English milkmaids, young girls who milked cows for a living, never got smallpox. They got cowpox, a mild disease from cows that produced pus-filled pockmarks like smallpox, but the disease passed in about six days and left no permanent scars. This put milkmaids in great demand as nurses who never got smallpox, and also as wives. The milkmaids had no smallpox scars on their faces, or anywhere else on their bodies, and had many suitors vying for their hands in marriage. Jenner ran some experiments by inoculating some milkmaids who had had cowpox and got mixed results. Sometimes the inoculation worked and sometimes not. At one time he talked so much about his studies that in dinner meetings with other area surgeons to exchange information about their occupation, he was forbidden to bring the subject up. Most felt the milkmaid story of smallpox immunity was simply farm gossip. But Jenner persisted, although he kept quiet among his friends about his efforts.

Jenner had decided that his prior problems were due to timing. If cowpox protected against smallpox, it was probably when the cowpox was at its peak. If it were past or before its peak strength, it would not give protection. Thus, the next time the disease came around in the spring of 1796, he was ready. A milkmaid named Sarah Nelmes got cowpox by milking an infected cow when her hand was previously scratched by the thorn of a rose. He took pus from a pustule on the girl's hand at the proper time (incidentally, a picture of the girl's hand with the pustule as well as the hide of the cow who gave her the cowpox is still preserved in museums), and on May 14, 1796, Jenner inoculated an eight-year-old boy named James Phipps with cowpox. The boy got cowpox and quickly recovered. The big test came on July 1, 1796, when Jenner then inoculated the boy with pus taken from a man with a case of smallpox. The boy never showed any sign of the disease. He had been protected by the cowpox.

It must be noted that Jenner was playing it safe in his mind at every step of the way. Inoculating the boy with cowpox seemed safe enough since there was no known record of anyone ever dying from cowpox. Then, inoculating the boy with smallpox pus was just what would have been done in the standard practice of inoculation. The boy was eight years old and was at high risk for smallpox because most children got smallpox by the age of seven. If the experiment failed the boy would have only gotten a harmless case of cowpox, and he would have been subject only to the standard risk of smallpox inoculation that hopefully would prevent him from getting a full-blown case of smallpox in any case.

In years to come Jenner would inoculate the boy 20 times just "to be sure." The boy never became ill in any way. The boy was the son of day laborers who often worked for Jenner, and in gratitude Jenner built the boy a cottage near Jenner's own house. The cottage still exists today as the Jenner Museum. Jenner continued with his experiments, finally vaccinating his own 18-month-old son in 1798.

Jenner was clearly aware of the implications of his experiments. He had given the world a way to protect against smallpox without having to actually inoculate anyone with the dreaded disease. The process became called "vaccination" after Jenner used the word "vaccine" for cowpox after the Latin word for cow. Jenner published several pamphlets about his work, and 70 years later the great Louis Pasteur would use the words "vaccine" and "vaccination" for any protective process of this sort against any disease to honor Jenner. The concept of vaccinating people to protect against a disease with a harmless vaccine became the standard technique in years to come. In Jenner's case he had stumbled across another disease (cowpox) that was harmless to humans but which made people immune to a very serious disease (smallpox). Eventually, after the concept of viruses was known, people would be vaccinated with killed or greatly weakened viruses of the same disease being protected against. These killed or weakened viruses would create immunity to the basic disease without harming the person being vaccinated (except in rare cases where a killed or weakened virus was not actually dead or weakened to the desired extent). We will have more to say about this when we discuss the elimination of polio in the 1950s by vaccination.

Back in 1800 there were many difficulties in getting Jenner's vaccination procedure into wide use. There were the usual protests about anything new that people in power often make to avoid any perceived threat to their power. These included doctors who had built up lucrative practices giving inoculations to people and saw vaccination as a threat to their business. There were the practical problems of transporting cowpox vaccine, which would only last a few days outside the host. Attempts to overcome this problem by giving arm-to-arm vaccinations (directly from a cowpox infected person to a new patient) ran into new problems when doctors realized that other diseases in an existing patient could be transferred to a new patient together with the vaccination material. For a while calves with cowpox were carried from place to place to permit vaccination of the masses. But all of these issues were slowly worked out and vaccination spread throughout the world. It would be about another 175 years before smallpox would be eradicated from the earth, as Jenner had forecast when he saw that his method worked. But his dream finally came true after a public health effort embracing the whole world through the United Nations eliminated smallpox as a disease in 1977.

The story of public health measures based on real medical breakthroughs in many nations started with the spread of vaccination against smallpox. But there had been other effective measures taken in public health before Jenner, and these measures were ongoing before other doctors and scientists developed the germ theory of disease between 1880 and 1900. This germ theory brought a new wave of understanding to the causes of disease and the methods by which they were spread. This information changed the basic directions of public health. Prior to Jenner and germ theory, most public health actions were based on watching who gets sick and who survives and defining actions accordingly, even if the causes of disease were still not specifically known. This period is often known as the age of the sanitarians.

The Age of the Sanitarians

In many respects, public health actions go back many centuries. The attempts of many cities to develop pure drinking water resulted in aqueducts being built in many places, including Rome. Reasonably sophisticated sewer systems were developed as well. No one knew for sure that infectious diseases were carried in impure drinking water, especially when contaminated by sewage disposal problems, but it was clear from experience that contaminated water of any kind seemed to cause problems. The same thing applied to food supplies. Further, the general process of moving from a hunter-gatherer society to an agricultural society brought the human race in much closer contact with each other and their domesticated animals. Infectious diseases could spread much more easily in such conditions, and the invention of the steam engine and the beginning on the Industrial Revolution in 1679 caused a long-term trend of movement to cities and crowded suburbs.

These crowded conditions made it even easier for diseases to spread and also caused the crowded, unsanitary conditions themselves to be viewed as the source of the diseases, even if there was no scientific proof of how the diseases were caused and spread. Thus, in England and in its colonies which would become the United States, the emphasis of public health before Jenner was on sanitation in terms of less crowding, more fresh air, cleaning up and draining swamps whose water and atmosphere were thought to breed disease, and in controlling private and public sewage systems so that they would not contaminate wells or other sources of drinking water. In a similar way, trash and garbage were not permitted to accumulate anywhere. It has been said that most public health officials in this period tended to work more closely with civil engineers than doctors. Also, in the United States where citizens were generally suspicious of central government and its laws, the towns and cities took the lead in public health efforts.

The impact of Jenner's work led to some changes in the concept of public health. In Boston in 1800, Dr. Benjamin Waterhouse, inspired by Jenner's writings, began to vaccinate children, including four of his own. The Boston Board of Health sent him some orphans to vaccinate as well. Waterford reported his good results to Thomas Jefferson, then president of the United States, and Jefferson had his family and slaves at his estate in Monticello, Virginia, vaccinated. When the Louisiana Purchase was made in 1803, Jefferson sent army surgeons to vaccinate Indians in the new territory. Unfortunately, money ran out before the program was completed, and the Indians would suffer from smallpox epidemics later in the decade. But as far as smallpox was concerned, vaccination became a public health issue that was widely accepted in the United States from 1800 onward. Otherwise, sanitation-oriented programs were the rule.

As noted before, sanitarian programs were often effective even if people did not always know why they worked. In fact, such famous sanitarians as Florence Nightingale in England and Surgeon General Dr. William Gorgas, of Panama Canal fame, in the United States, believed that overcrowded, unsanitary conditions were the key to producing disease, even after they knew about the germ theory of disease by 1900. Nightingale was an independently wealthy British socialite who became famous when she went to a British military hospital in Scutari, Turkey, in 1854, during the Crimean War. She and her crew of nurses greatly reduced the death rate in the hospital primarily through a regime of soap and water, less crowding, and nourishing food. She later wrote and taught in London and became an icon of the sanitary movement. Nightingale refused to accept the germ theory of disease that was developed by the end of the 1800s, and she even went so far as to state that there was only one infectious disease process. It was made steadily worse when people, already suffering from poor nutrition, were forced to live in crowded, unsanitary conditions. This is an example of how someone so completely wrong about the actual cause of disease still did a lot of good in the area of public health as a result of her dedicated efforts to promote programs that actually worked regardless of the theory behind them.

Gorgas, who is credited with greatly reducing deaths from malaria and yellow fever in the time of the Spanish-America War and the building of the Panama Canal circa 1900, later stated that his success at the canal was due to moving the bulk of the work force (mostly blacks from Jamaica and the West Indies) from crowded and unsanitary barracks-type housing to individual free-standing cabins and huts. While controlling the mosquitoes — known by then to carry malaria and yellow fever — was a factor, Gorgas said the key canal problem was actually pneumonia that spread readily in the crowded and dirty barracks. Gorgas was convinced that filth rather than mosquitoes was the cause of yellow fever (to which he was immune after having the disease in childhood), and he made Havana one of the cleanest cities in the world following the war in 1898. He accepted the fact that at the Panama Canal in 1906 the pneumococci microbe produced pneumonia, but he still felt that improved nutrition and better sanitation was the key to controlling the disease.

During the general emphasis on sanitation in the seventeenth and especially the eighteenth century, there was also a notable development in the related areas of personal hygiene and cleaner conditions in hospitals. Oliver Wendell Holmes Sr., now known mainly for his poetry in the United States, was originally trained as a physician. In 1843, he published an essay that blamed puerperal (childbirth) fever on the doctors attending women in labor and treating their patients without proper precautions of such simple things as washing their hands and wearing clean clothing. Holmes quoted in his essay several other doctors who had similar opinions, some of whom had spoken out in the past. The essay drew considerable opposition from doctors who considered their hands to be as sacred as their profession and who were outraged to be told that they were the cause of spreading disease. Holmes had no taste for controversy and basically withdrew into his writing activities.

But another doctor in Hungary, Ignaz Philipp Semmelweis, took up the battle in 1846. He blamed the deadly fever on doctors who went straight from performing autopsies to duty in the maternity wards and then went from patient to patient, all without washing their hands. Semmelweis established rules in wards under his command requiring careful and consistent washing of hands with soap and rinsing with chlorinated water before touching patients. The rates of puerperal fell dramatically, and his procedures attracted great attention.

However, Semmelweis was a difficult man, and he persisted in calling doctors who failed to follow his recommendations assassins and murderers. Some doctors felt puerperal fever was just another random infectious disease and ridiculed Semmelweis' ideas, especially when he blamed the spread of the ugly fever on them. Actually the results of Semmelweis' work began to speak for themselves, and many doctors began to follow the policies of chemical antisepsis, just as Holmes and others had urged previously. Ironically, the more his teachings took hold, the more Semmelweis personally was attacked (and vice versa). Semmelweis died in a mental hospital in 1865 under controversial conditions. But at the same time, an English surgeon named Joseph Lister would find a theoretical basis for antiseptic procedures in hospitals. The great sanitary movement based on faith in sanitation would slowly come to a close as scientific principles took over.

Lister was greatly frustrated as a surgeon because in most cases of surgery, the patient would die from infection of the surgical wound (many patients in hospitals in those days died from infections contracted there regardless of their reason for being hospitalized). Lister was familiar with the work of Semmelweis and later gave him much credit, but at the time Lister seemed not to make a connection between the results Semmelweis obtained and the problems of surgical infection.

But Lister did take notice of articles published by Louis Pasteur, the great French scientist who was a transitory link from the sanitary movement to the germ theory of disease. Pasteur was basically a chemist, and in his early work proved that bacteria and such (as had been seen in an early microscope starting in the 1600s) were always present in the air and would cause fermentation/putrefaction (the basis of Pasteur's development of pasteurization of milk). Pasteur did much more than this in his career, and we will return to his overall accomplishments later. The work that caught Lister's eye had to do with getting rid of these organisms by filtering, heating, or using chemicals. Lister had believed the current theories that he had been taught that claimed infections leading to gangrene were due to some reaction between oxygen and the blood. When Lister learned from Pasteur that microbes freely floating in the atmosphere caused infection (and putrefaction, gangrene, and the rest), Lister realized that even if it were impossible to avoid oxygen, it was possible to avoid germs by filtering or to kill them outright with heat or chemicals. He immediately began to look for a chemical that would kill microbes but not harm the patient.

Lister started in 1865 with carbolic acid (phenol), which had been used by sanitarians to kill the stench arising from sewage (the sanitarians believed the stench itself was the cause of infectious disease). He cleaned his instruments and the surgical area with carbolic acid and dressed the wound with dressings soaked in carbolic acid. After some experimentation to determine the proper concentration and methods of application, the results were remarkable. Soon Lister required all attendees to wear clean gloves and to vigorously wash their hands in carbolic acid. He even had it sprayed around the operating room. He published articles of his results in May 1867.

Almost on cue, many of his peers laughed at him. However, Lister simply shrugged off those he called too stupid to understand. Many of his critics still thought germs arose from "spontaneous generation." But Lister quickly got support in the real world. In the Franco-Prussian War of 1870, military surgeons on both sides used what they called "Listerism" to reduce deaths due to the infection of wounds requiring surgery. As a result, in postwar Germany and France, Lister was a hero, and most surgeons and hospitals in these countries followed his techniques.

Lister's fame and recognition grew more slowly in Britain, but by 1877 he was appointed professor of surgery at King's College in London and became the top surgeon in the country. His techniques spread around the world, and in a trivial way that still demonstrated the homage paid to his name, Listerine mouthwash was named after him and became widely familiar in the United States. Lister's work gave the final push to the urgings of sanitarians and helped turn hospitals into the clean and healing places they are today, with the trace of various disinfectants in the air. Prior to this, many hospitals had been the source of deadly infections for patients rather than a place of healing. The stage was now set for the introduction of the germ theory of disease.

The Era of the Germ Theory of Disease

The era of the germ theory of disease reached its climax between 1880 and 1900, but the beginnings were a few decades earlier. Actually, although the work of Louis Pasteur in France beginning around 1850 can be considered the start of the germ theory, the work of Antony van Leeuwenhoek and his microscopes in the late 1660s has to be credited with also playing a big role.

Leeuwenhoek did not invent the microscope, as many believe. Microscopes, including compound versions (units with more than one lens) were available in the 1500s, as many as 40 years before Leeuwenhoek was born in 1632. Leeuwenhoek, a man of many trades (none of which related to science or medicine), learned to grind lenses in the 1660s, and he began experimenting with his own simple microscopes and looking at drops of water and similar things. This had been done previously using compound microscopes, but construction difficulties limited compound units to magnifications of 20 or 30 times. Leeuwenhoek's skill at grinding lenses, his great natural eyesight, and his ability to carefully adjust the light enabled him to achieve magnifications of more than 200. In 1673, Leeuwenhoek began to send letters and drawings describing what he had been seeing with his microscope to the recently formed Royal Society of London, an organization dedicated to science. Leeuwenhoek sent such letters for the next 50 years until his death just before the age of 91 in 1723. The letters were immensely popular and were published in the official transactions of the society and in many reprints.

The significance of Leeuwenhoek's work was that the examination of various items to determine the types of bacteria and other organisms that were present became the norm in scientific and medical research. There were many different opinions about the meaning of these bacteria and how they came to be there. But no one could fail to admit that they existed.

Louis Pasteur was a leader in determining how the bacteria happened to exist in the views under the microscope and what their presence meant in terms of disease. Pasteur was not a doctor and had limited formal medical training, although his discoveries revolutionized the field of medicine. Pasteur was primarily trained as a chemist, and his original plan was to become a teacher in the field. When Pasteur was appointed professor of chemistry at the University of Lille in 1854 at the age of 32, he included in his opening address to the students a phrase that defined his approach to his work: "Chance favors only the mind that is prepared." Pasteur also stated: "Without theory, practice is but routine born of habit. Theory alone can bring forth and develop the spirit of invention." Pasteur was not encumbered by any preconceived notions of how things worked. He was prepared to accept — and to look for — any new discoveries that he could make under his microscope.

In a similar vein, Pasteur readily accepted the urgings of the French political ministry to focus his research on the needs of local industry rather than scholarly research. Pasteur was a pragmatist and set out to help the local brewing industry as requested. Pasteur had already discovered several years earlier that tartrate acid crystals had molecular dissymmetry that explained the differences they demonstrated to polarized light. This finding helped distillers of industrial alcohol avoid the adverse effects that molds feeding and growing on tartrates might have on fermentation.

Pasteur set out at Lille to study fermentation in more detail. He confirmed that yeast was a living organism, and he developed a way for brewers to avoid failures in fermentation in making wine. This method involved gentle heating during the fermentation process to eliminate undesirable bacteria that arose during the process. Pasteur experimented with many forms of fermentation, and his process of heating to destroy unwanted bacteria became called pasteurization. We apply the term primarily to milk, but it was actually a universal technique. It led to a revolution in medicine, because many others saw, as did Pasteur, that the process had implications in infections and even infectious disease. If bacteria caused these problems in the fermentation process, bacteria could cause infections in wounds, because the putrefaction process was much like the fermentation process.

The doctors who avoided accepting this idea most vigorously were those who believed that bacteria arose from "spontaneous generation" as the result of some mysterious reaction with air. Pasteur refuted this theory in a dramatic demonstration in 1864 before the members of the Academy of Sciences. He prepared flasks full of a freshly boiled nutrient broth. Then he admitted air to the flasks through an intricate series of glass tubing. One system had a filter that would not admit passage of bacteria, and one system was cleverly arranged so that air could pass through, but not the tiny dust particles to which bacteria were thought to cling. Nothing grew in the nutrient broths. Pasteur had overthrown with one stroke the theory of spontaneous generation. His intent was simply to remove a barrier to the germ theory of disease, which he now firmly believed was the basis for all form of infection and infectious disease. Soon after this demonstration by Pasteur, Joseph Lister in Britain started his revolution in septic surgery as a result of reading Pasteur's publications.

In 1865 Pasteur interrupted his ongoing work on fermentation and related processes to respond to a request for help once more from local industry, this time silkworm growers. Over the next three years, Pasteur showed that two different parasitic organisms were attacking the silkworms, and he derived methods to control them. His work was not only of great economic significance, but it contributed to the concept of the germ theory of disease, and many other scientists and doctors made advancements in the field while Pasteur was hampered by a stroke that paralyzed the left side of his body in 1868.

Pasteur recovered enough from his stroke to develop a vaccine for chicken cholera by using a greatly weakened strain of the bacteria that caused chicken cholera as a vaccine. The discovery came partly due to a fortuitous accident in the summer of 1879 when old infectious material was found not to cause the cholera. But Pasteur had the prepared mind that chance favors, and he recognized quickly what had happened. He worked how much the deadly material needed to be weakened to turn it into a vaccine, and chicken cholera was no longer a deadly disease for chickens. Again Pasteur's work was both economically and theoretically significant. Pasteur realized he had discovered the first vaccine since Jenner used cowpox as a safe protective against smallpox 83 years earlier in 1796. Pasteur used the word "vaccine" in honor of Jenner, and thereafter everyone used the term to describe an inoculation made with a protective material to prevent an infectious disease, even though later efforts were really only an analog to Jenner's process.

In 1880, Pasteur used heat to alter (but not completely kill) anthrax bacteria and thus developed a vaccine for anthrax in animals, mainly sheep. Again, almost on cue, veterinarians derided his work. But in 1881 public trials were held in which anthrax was given to vaccinated and non-vaccinated animals. Every vaccinated animal survived and every non-vaccinated animal died. Veterinarians stopped their derision and raced off to meet the demand of farmers to vaccinate over 20,000 sheep and other animals in the areas around Paris within two weeks after the public trials were completed.

A key to Pasteur's work was his ability to work diligently under his microscope. He doggedly isolated the microorganisms that caused sour tastes in non-pasteurized products and that caused disease in silkworms and farm animals. Then he was able to find a way to destroy these microorganisms or to develop a vaccine to protect against future attacks. Pasteur at least could see his enemies and figure out how to dispatch or protect against them. His hero, Jenner, had complained that because of a lack of knowledge about how things worked, it was natural for doctors to stumble around in the dark like coal miners in a dark mine without a headlamp. But Jenner had been taught by his mentor to experiment when he was unsure. And so he did, with great results. Pasteur was surer of what was happening based on his work (and that of his peers) under the microscope, and Pasteur as well was willing to experiment. Pasteur's next experiment brought him perhaps his greatest fame.

Pasteur next turned to the study of rabies. Rabies was not a common disease, but it was greatly feared. There was no known cure for rabies, and persons or animals bitten by an animal having the disease were condemned to a horrific death (even today, untreated rabies is 100 percent fatal). At the time, no one had yet isolated the microbe responsible for causing the disease. It had been studied for some time, but little was known about the disease except that it had an incubation period of several weeks after one was bitten. Pasteur was personally familiar with this fact. As a nine-year-old he witnessed a young man bitten by a rabid wolf (which had caused eight other deaths in the small community) have his wound immediately cauterized with a red-hot poker by a blacksmith. The young man survived with only a terrible scar. Pasteur later realized that this cauterization had killed the rabies venom long before its incubation period, and the rabies never developed in the young man.

Pasteur worked for four years without being able to isolate the cause of rabies, which happens to be a virus. A virus was unable to be seen at the time and generally unknown in medicine. But by 1884 Pasteur was able to at least discern the difference between animal spinal-cord tissues that were rabid and those that were not. With this as a measure, Pasteur worked out a series of inoculations, starting with rabies-causing material that was old (14 days or so) and working up to a relatively fresh and virulent material that would no longer produce rabies in the animal being tested. He surmised, correctly, that while a new attack of rabies was still in the incubation stage, a victim could develop immunity from the series of shots so that the body could defeat the new rabies while it was still in the incubation process. In other words, although he didn't know about the process, the immune system had developed enough antibodies to defeat a new attack of rabies.

Pasteur ran a series of animal tests and was sure his new vaccine would work, even though the vaccine was more a cure than a preventive. But a trial on humans would be a daunting step. He considered trying to arrange a process in which condemned convicts would be offered life in prison rather than death for becoming "volunteers" for such a test. However, fate intervened and the vaccine was soon put to a human test. On July 4, 1885, a nine-year-old boy named Joseph Meister was bitten in Alsace by a rabid dog while he was on his way to school. The local doctor, who was familiar with Pasteur's work, told the boy's mother to take the boy to Paris to see Pasteur because it was felt to be his only chance to survive. Pasteur was not officially a doctor, so he enlisted the help of two doctors when the boy arrived in Paris two days later. They officially prescribed Pasteur's vaccination process because they also felt it was the boy's only hope. By July 27 the boy had not developed hydrophobia or any other fatal symptoms of rabies, and he was sent home.

Ironically, this happy event essentially ended Pasteur's career as a researcher. The news of Pasteur's latest triumph caused a sensation around the world. Patients and reporters poured into Paris, and by 1888 public subscriptions and government funds had created the Pasteur Institute that Pasteur headed until his death in 1895. Pasteur's birthday became a national holiday, and to a large extent Pasteur spent his last years as a celebrity rather than a research scientist.

There were many doctors and scientists involved in developing the germ theory of disease between 1880 and 1900, but Pasteur stands not only as a leading experimenter on his own but as an inspiration to many others to take up this field of study. Pasteur's development of the process of pasteurization, a word we often use today without a thought about the person in whose honor it was named, and his related work in this area was really the start of the germ theory of disease. Pasteur brought vaccination far beyond Edward Jenner's trailblazing work at the end of the previous century in 1796. Pasteur started everyone thinking in terms of obtaining a vaccine for all known infectious diseases.

Perhaps the best summary of Pasteur's contributions was written by Sir William Osler, a professor of medicine at John Hopkins in Baltimore and later the Regis Professor of Medicine at Oxford, who wrote the widely used textbook *Principles and Practice of Medicine*. In 1900 Osler was asked to write the introduction to the English-language version of Pasteur's official biography (written by Pasteur's son-in-law who was a doctor). Osler wrote that "Pasteur's work constituted three great discoveries" which were that "Each fermentation is produced by the development of a special microbe; Each infectious disease is produced by the development within the organism of a special microbe; The microbe of an infectious disease culture, under certain detrimental conditions, is attenuated in its pathogenic activity — from a virus it has become a vaccine." This last sentence by Osler was essentially one of hope because it would take some years to obtain good vaccines after Pasteur's work, even though the causative microbes of most diseases would be isolated by 1900.

For the record, the causative microbes for the following diseases were isolated between 1880 and 1898: leprosy and malaria in 1880; tuberculosis and glanders in 1882; cholera in 1883; diphtheria, typhoid, staphylococcus, streptococcus, and tetanus in 1884; coli in 1885; pneumococcus in 1886; Malta fever and soft chancre in 1887; gas gangrene in 1892; plague and botulism in 1894; and dysentery in 1898. This list basically swept aside all objections to the germ theory of disease, and public health issues in the United States from 1900 onward were focused on developing vaccines for diseases caused by microbes. There were also efforts to take public actions to reduce the spread of diseases now that their causes (and in most cases their methods of transmission) were subjects of hard fact, rather than speculation.

As part of these efforts, a bacteriological laboratory was set up under federal auspices in the 1890s in Washington, D.C. to research and test various serums, vaccines, and related products. Notable state health department laboratories were established in 1888 by Charles V. Chaplin in Providence, Rhode Island, and by Victor V. Vaughn in Michigan. These state laboratories were primarily for the analysis and screening of water and food. The efforts in Rhode Island and Michigan became models for many other states.

But the major initiative in public health at this time was made in the New York City Department of Health. Hermann M. Biggs was the leader of this effort. Following the establishment of a screening laboratory in 1892 to be sure no harmful elements entered New York as the result of a cholera outbreak in Hamburg, Germany, the city converted the laboratory to focus on the control of diphtheria. Doctor William H. Park was placed in charge of the program and was primarily responsible for the development about 20 years later of a vaccine against diphtheria that is now part of the DPT series of vaccines given today to all children. The laboratory became a research vehicle to study other diseases, and many state and local health boards later followed the example set by the New York City Board of Health.

However, it must be noted that epidemics of such infectious diseases as yellow fever and cholera declined sharply in the United States even before the microbe producing them had been identified. This was primarily an end result of the great sanitation movement and its theme that "a clean city is a healthy city." Including this effort with the new information made available from the germ theory discoveries improved public health, especially as measured by such things as infant mortality. For example, in New York City alone, infant mortality fell from a rate of 273 per 1,000 live births in 1885 to a level of 94 per 1,000 live births in 1915. This 66 percent decline was believed at the time to be primarily due to improvements in the water and milk supplies achieved as a result of sanitation procedures and bacteriological screening.

Before discussing the major medical advances that were made in chemotherapy and antibiotics in the 1920s through the early 1940s, which led to the next upward movement in public health, we should discuss the great flu/pneumonia epidemic of 1918–1919 that struck the United States (and the world as a whole). This epidemic put great strains on the public health system that had evolved so well in the United States from the late 1800s and early 1900s. This epidemic caused more deaths from infectious disease in the United States than had any prior epidemic (or any epidemic since).

The Great Flu/Pneumonia Epidemic of 1918–1919

The great epidemic of 1918–1919 is more properly called a pandemic because it killed as many as an estimated 30 million people around the world, including the half million or so killed in the United States. But this is as good a place as any in this chronology to make a split between public health in the rest of the world and public health in the United States. The discoveries that followed the development of the germ theory of disease, and the coming of antibiotics in the twentieth century, made the level of public health achieved in the United States following the sanitarian era far different than in the rest of the world, except in certain isolated areas like Western Europe, England, and modern Japan. Infectious diseases considered now to be only minor issues in the United States are still great killers in much of the rest of the world, for both sanitary and medical reasons. Public health today in the United States must focus on the diseases of aging like cardiovascular disease and cancer. Infectious diseases are comparatively small causes of death rather than great killers for most Americans today, and our death rates from various causes and our resultant life expectancies (to be discussed later in this introduction as the proper measure of public health) have little relevance to much of the rest of the world. Accordingly, we will discuss the flu/pneumonia epidemic of 1918–1919 primarily from the viewpoint of happenings in the United States.

The flu/pneumonia epidemic that rose to prominence in the fall of 1918 was exacerbated by the fact that the United States had entered World War I in the spring of 1917 and was sending great numbers of soldiers to Europe in the fall of 1918. Military camps were everywhere, and the crowded and often unsanitary conditions, including those on many troopships, were ideal for the spread of any disease, especially one like flu, which could be spread by droplets in the air carrying the tiny viruses that cause the disease. Military troops were mixed widely within the population, especially in large port cities near training camps and embarkation points. The military orientation of the disease was shown by the fact that the then-relatively isolated interior parts of the country were not initially affected, although in time all parts of the country were involved.

The disease became known as the "Spanish flu," but some analysts said that was only because Spain, as a non-combatant in the war, was not subject to severe censorship of its newspapers that accurately published the news of the epidemic there. European combatants and the United States could not report as freely on such items, and Spain was improperly identified in some places as having the disease first and/or to the greatest extent. The real source of the flu, as is often the case even today, was probably China. The flu virus easily moves between humans and pigs and birds, and China, as the country with a large, if not the largest, population of each, often produces new strains that then move around the world. There had been some pneumonia plague outbreaks in Manchuria between 1910 and 1917 (similar to the black death of medieval history), and maybe that epidemic had triggered a 1918 outburst of an unusually virulent flu/pneumonia combination.

The first serious flu alarm in 1918 occurred in September at Camp Devens near Boston, Massachusetts. Dr. William Henry Welch, a distinguished physician and pathologist who had been president of several medical associations, including the American Medical Association (AMA), and who had left John Hopkins to join the army and help the army surgeon general inspect the crowded army camps. Military leaders knew that in all previous wars, more American soldiers died of disease than in actual combat, and they were trying to avoid the spread of infectious diseases this time. Dr. Welch was sent to investigate horror stories coming in from the Boston area about Spanish flu.

Dr. Welch was soon to learn that this flu was unlike any he had ever seen. In fact, one of the most notable things about the flu in 1918 was that it had a propensity for pneumonia complications unlike any flu ever known before (or since). This was crucial because while flu may make you feel miserable for a few days, pneumonia kills. When Dr. Welch performed autopsies on dead soldiers (while new bodies were being stacked around him like cordwood), he was amazed at the horrible condition of the men's lungs. At first he thought a new form of disease or plague had arisen.

What Dr. Welch saw was to become the hallmark of the epidemic. The key victims were young adults who should have been in the prime of life, rather than the very young and very old who normally suffered most from flu outbreaks. No one knew what to do about the flu in terms of a cure. The only methods known to help were to avoid overcrowding and direct contact with existing carriers. This method was nearly impossible to put into effect in the military, especially as there were signs that the fresh troops from the United States were beginning to turn the tide of battle in Europe. The only thing to do, as it turned out, was to hunker down and try to stop the spread of the disease until it went away. That essentially was what the country did for the rest of 1918, and in spite of increased cases of the disease in the first part of 1919, it did eventually go away. Even today no one knows how it started, why it went away, and if it may someday come back. In the United States there would be new weapons to battle the disease with if it returned, but no one knows if it would return in the same form.

Philadelphia was an example of an East Coast city that seemed reasonably well prepared for the flu to come after the Massachusetts experience. But many Philadelphia public health and hospital personnel were away at the war, and when a full-scale outbreak of flu/pneumonia occurred in October 1918, the city was overwhelmed. However, the city finally got its act together to fight back. Parades and such went on to support liberty loan drives to fund the war in spite of the danger of spreading the flu at such occasions, but otherwise intelligent actions were taken. When the relatively new phone system was overloaded with calls for help, a number identified as Filbert 100 was established to take calls about nothing but the flu 24 hours a day. A preliminary visit was made that provided information and simple services, and the number of calls referred to the all-too-busy medical services were reduced by a third. Schools and places of entertainment were closed, and even church services were banned. Volunteers from everywhere and nearly every civil and religious organization were pressed into service to help, including drivers to take the ill to hospitals and the dead to morgues and cemeteries, which similarly used volunteers to dig graves. By the end of October the flu surge seemed to be over, and the city returned more or less to normal just in time to celebrate the end of the war on November 11, 1918. There were 12,162 deaths from flu/pneumonia reported between the weeks ending October 5 and November 2, with a peak of 4,597 reported for the week ending October 19. There was a resurgence of flu in February 1919, but deaths were less than a tenth of the October rate, and the city managed to cope.

San Francisco was an example of a West Coast port city that was also devastated for a time by the flu, but the overall response included a controversial item, the wearing of surgical masks, that finally split the citizens. San Francisco had two epidemic peaks, one in 1918 and a second in early 1919. San Francisco in 1918 had a population of about 550,000, roughly only a third of that of Philadelphia. San Francisco had early warning about the flu, and its chief of the board of health, Dr. William Hassler, ordered quarantine against the naval training camps in the Bay Area. In early October, tens of thousands took part in a number of parades and activities supporting San Francisco's fourth liberty loan bond drive.

In proper precautionary measures, Dr. Hassler met with hospital officials and moved all patients out of the San Francisco hospital to be able to use it as an isolation unit for flu patients only. Other hospitals accepted the moved patients and also instituted a policy of refusing new minor cases until the coming flu epidemic passed. All seemed well prepared, but the city approached chaos, as had happened elsewhere, when the flu hit in earnest.

By October 14, a total of 991 cases of flu had been reported, including 378 on that day. In the week ending October 19, over 4,000 new cases were reported with 130 deaths. The board of health issued a closing order to close down schools, places of public gatherings, and places of amusement. Church services were forbidden two days later. In spite of the preparations, hospital services were overrun, and a makeshift hospital for children was set up in the civic auditorium. There were shortages of caregivers of all types, and chaos ruled until the epidemic peaked on October 25, when a total of 2,319 new cases were reported.

In the 60 days since September 23, over 23,558 cases of flu had been reported; these numbers were probably well below the actual total. In October alone 1,067 had died. Many other eastern cities had done much worse, and there was a sense of self-congratulation, as the flu seemed to go away with the announcement of the end of the war in November. All the closed places slowly reopened, and the public schools were back in business by November 25. Dr. Hassler had begun a program in October to inoculate citizens with a flu vaccine brought in from the east. Of course the so-called vaccine was useless, as no one had found a true vaccine at the time. Still, the attitude was that it couldn't do any harm, and the epidemic did seem to fade as the vaccinations increased.

What gave a semi-comic tone to the serious epidemic was the issue of the wearing of surgical masks, like those worn in hospitals. An ordinance was passed in San Francisco during the height of the epidemic requiring the wearing of the masks because Dr. Hassler was convinced of their value. The tiny flu virus could easily pass through such masks, although motes of dust and droplets of water on which a virus might be riding could be caught by the mask. The masks would have to be worn all the time to be effective, but they were normally worn outside where air currents were vigorous and then removed in a crowded restaurant or other such place where they were most needed.

Citizens were arrested for not wearing their masks, and in some cases they took to wearing them on their ears or the buttons of their coats to meet the letter of the law. The celebration of the ending of the war had a surreal atmosphere with mask-wearing citizens waving and shouting happily. The flu rate fell sharply once masks were used in earnest in late October, and Hassler insisted this was more than happy coincidence. Finally, on November 21, the ordnance was repealed, and the citizens of San Francisco could legally go on their errands without a mask for the first time in a month. Hassler wanted people to continue wearing the masks, but most citizens had had enough of the inconvenient practice.

However, as December got underway, it was clear that the number of flu cases was beginning to rise ominously. Dr. Hassler immediately recommended that the masks be taken up again, and the mayor agreed and issued a non-binding proclamation accordingly. But the mask magic was gone. People were tired of them and pointed out the incongruity of wearing them outside where they were less needed and removing them inside in crowded areas where they were needed most — if in fact they really worked. The board of health even stated on December 18 that the new situation did not require such "extraordinary" measures as masking. In addition, Dr. F. L. Kelly, of the bacteriological laboratory of the University of California, stated "we don't know any more about the disease today than we did a hundred years ago. There is no known cure or preventative."

Dr. Hassler was unconvinced, and after a series of battles with the board of supervisors, got them to edict masking again on January 17, 1919. Amazingly, the rate of new cases began immediately to decline. But the health officer of San Mateo county, just south of San Francisco where no masks were required, pointed out that the flu had ebbed just as it had in San Francisco. Even the head of the state board of health said that masks were ineffective and that 78 percent of the nurses at San Francisco Hospital had gotten the flu in the fall even though they all wore masks and he considered that hospital to be one of the best run with the most disciplined staff in the state. He added that the city of Stockton, where masks had be worn most faithfully and consistently of any city in the state, had the same death rate as the city of Boston back east, and Boston had staggered through its epidemic with a minimum of preventatives of any kind.

As the number of new cases continued to fall, the board of health advised the mayor of San Francisco to proclaim that it was safe to drop the masks on February 1, 1919. Those who supported the use of masks could say (accurately) that the data confirmed their position. When the masks went on in the fall, the rate of new flu cases declined. When the masks came off, the flu rate increased again, then declined as masks were mandated again in January. However, as some doctors claimed then, and we know now, the masks, especially as used in San Francisco, had little if any effect on the disease. One could just as easily say that the flu epidemic had an odd effect in San Francisco. When the flu peaked in the fall of 1918, citizens appeared in white masks. When it declined in December, the masks disappeared. The cycle was repeated in the early months of 1919.

The San Francisco battle over the use of masks is indicative of the problems of carrying out effective public health measures. Success requires full cooperation of the citizens, and there must be some believable scientific connection between the measure recommended and the expected result. The Salk vaccine against polio in the early 1950s is a good example of an immensely successful public health measure. Parents were terrified of the crippling effects of the disease on their children, there was a scientific connection to fall back on, and initial trials were successful. Accordingly, parents agreed by the millions to have their children vaccinated, and polio disappeared as a threat. Today, there are good scientific connections to identify smoking and poor diet and exercise regimes as the true leading causes of death in the United States, but young adults find it hard to believe they are ever going to die of anything, and people at all ages find it hard to diet and exercise for a potential benefit of extended life. Thus, public health educational programs in these areas are qualified successes, at best. However, the anti-smoking programs have cut the number of adult smokers, even as younger smokers constantly take up the habit.

The flu/pneumonia epidemic of 1918–19 was to a large extent a demonstration that cities in the United States were able to muddle through a fast-moving epidemic, against which they had no real medical defense, by using public-spirited volunteers directed by a still-developing public health organization. As will be shown later, the death rate in the nation peaked at a level never approached before or since in 1918–19, but the nation carried on and the epidemic was largely quickly forgotten.

The Coming of Chemotherapy and Antibiotics

Although vaccines were slowly being developed at the beginning of the twentieth century as preventatives against the most common infectious diseases, the real miracle of the twentieth century was long considered to be the development of antibiotic drugs that would kill infectious diseases after they had infected a patient. At one time, these drugs were considered to mark the end of concern over infectious diseases based on the actions of bacteria, but it was learned old infectious diseases could develop immunity to old drugs. New versions of these infectious diseases would require new drugs. It must also be noted that antibiotics meant exactly that — drugs that would work to kill diseases that were caused in some way by bacteria. Such drugs would not work against viruses, which had no life cycle of their own, but which took over existing human cells to reproduce. Thus, the battle against diseases was far from won, and the final outcome is still unknown.

The first notable use of chemotherapy to develop an antibiotic drug happened in 1910 when Paul Ehrlich, a German doctor who was also a public health officer in Frankfurt, came up with what he called Salvarsan, the first drug that was effective against syphilis. The drug was initially popularly known as Salvarsan 606, because it was the 606th in a series of arsenic-based drugs being methodically tested in Ehrlich's laboratory for various purposes. The drug was actually developed in 1907 and set aside when it proved ineffective for the purpose for which it was intended. But when it was tested again against the spirochete that was recently isolated as the cause of syphilis, it became the magic bullet Ehrlich was seeking — a chemical that attacks the disease without harming other tissues. Ehrlich had figured out that the immune system worked this way, and his techniques were actually the beginning of chemotherapy. We now associate that word with cancer treatments, but at the time Ehrlich was looking for chemicals that would emulate the immune system and prove therapeutic against specific diseases. Hence the name chemotherapy.

Pasteur had been looking for a chemical vaccine late in his life that would prevent disease just as weakened viruses served as a vaccine against the same virus, as in the case of his anthrax vaccine. Ehrlich was involved in related fields in the 1880s and 1890s, and although few know his name today, Ehrlich was just as towering a figure as Pasteur had been.

Ehrlich did a great deal of work in discovering how the immune system works, and he should be credited with starting the field of immunology as well as getting researchers started in chemotherapy. He also did important work in determining that the deadly effect of certain bacteria was due to toxins created by these bacteria, and he helped in developing antitoxins that eventually led to a cure for and a vaccine against diphtheria, among other diseases. Many other people helped these events to fruition, but Ehrlich was ahead of his time in immunology and chemotherapy and was the creative force behind much important work done in these fields in the late nineteenth century and the early twentieth century (studies that are still going on).

The next big step in antibiotics came in 1936 when scientists at John Hopkins University developed many derivatives of sulfanilamide, or the sulfa drugs. These drugs had their origin in 1908 when they were developed as a red dye for wool. In 1932, it was found that a similar synthetic drug had antagonistic properties against a wide range of bacteria. Work at Johns Hopkins found that the sulfa drugs did not kill bacteria per se, but they interfered with the metabolic processes of the bacteria and stopped their growth. Then the natural defenses of the immune system could gain the upper hand. Various versions of the sulfa drugs turned out to be useful in treating pneumonia, meningitis, peritonitis, syphilis, gonorrhea, and other diseases. The sulfa drugs had some toxic side effects, but if used under careful medical supervision, they were a new weapon in the fight against infectious diseases caused by bacteria.

Penicillin, the ultimate antibiotic drug at the time (and for many years after) was discovered in 1928 in Britain by Alexander Fleming, but it was not turned into a useful drug until 1944. A young French medical student actually discovered it first in 1896, but his work was forgotten. Fleming rediscovered it by accident in 1928 when he noticed something had fallen into a petri dish and was killing bacteria he was keeping there. He identified the killing material as a mold named *Penicillum notarium* and purified and isolated the active ingredient that he called penicillin. Fleming ran some tests, but he wasn't sure penicillin would last long enough in the human body to be really effective, and at any rate he had no means of producing in large quantities. He published his results and hoped someone would follow up his research, but no one did.

Later in the 1930s as World War II approached, British researchers Walter Flory and Ernst Chain were looking for ways to prevent infection from battlefield wounds. With a well-stocked laboratory at Oxford, they came across Fleming's paper, went to visit him, and came back with a sample of penicillin Fleming had kept alive for a decade by transferring it from petri dish to petri dish. Flory and Chain confirmed Fleming's work, developed a way to mass-produce the penicillin, and took it to the United States where it was turned out in huge amounts. Large numbers of wounded soldiers were saved in World War II, and penicillin became a cheap, easily produced drug that was to save millions of civilian lives as well. In 1945, Fleming, Flory, and Chain shared the Nobel Prize in medicine for their efforts in the development of penicillin.

As an antibiotic, penicillin works against a number of infectious diseases by either preventing the bacteria from dividing or causing their death if they tried. Dorothy Hodgkin of Britain completely determined the atomic structure of penicillin in 1945, and this permitted it to be manufactured synthetically. Penicillin and its many derivatives is by far the most common drug used against infectious diseases, but in spite of hopes it would be the crowning achievement of mankind in the bacterial wars, mutated strains of bacteria have developed that are resistant to penicillin. The man/bacteria battle seems likely to go on forever.

The final antibiotic victory in this period came with the development of streptomycin in 1945. Penicillin was not effective against what were called gram-negative bacteria, based on the way bacteria reacted when stained with iodine and later washed with alcohol. This technique had been developed many years before to help see bacteria clearly under a microscope, and it became a useful way to classify bacteria based on whether the bacteria remained stained (gram positive) or lost the stain (gram negative).

Selman Waksman was born in Russia but emigrated to the United States, received a degree in agriculture from Rutgers in 1915, and later received a Ph.D. in biochemistry in 1918 from the University of California. During the next 20 years he published nearly 400 papers on how microorganisms gave fertility to the soil, and he became an expert on soil microbiology. When details on penicillin became available in 1939, he realized it was not a universal antibiotic (a word he has been credited with coining). Unfortunately, one of the gram-negative bacteria not sensitive to penicillin was the one that caused tuberculosis. But Waksman had also noticed in his work that the tuberculosis microbe did not survive in soil.

Waksman and his staff made a methodical survey of more than 10,000 microorganisms found in soil. In 1943, he found the item killing the tuberculosis microbe was in a mold of the streptomycin family, a mold he had been growing for research purposes for nearly 20 years. He extracted an antibiotic from the mold in 1945 and named it streptomycin. It was effective against tuberculosis and other diseases caused by gram-negative bacteria, including some forms of pneumonia as well as spinal meningitis and typhoid fever. Waksman continued to work with the mold and isolated several other antibiotics, including neomycin. Waksman won the 1952 Nobel Prize in medicine for his work.

With these three basic drugs in hand (sulfas, penicillin, and streptomycin), a basic armament had been created against infectious bacterial diseases. Many versions of these drugs would follow, and in the United States, at least, such infectious diseases would become minor causes of death despite the need to overcome versions of the diseases that had become resistant to the original drugs. The next step would be to develop some new vaccines to fight against diseases caused by viruses, which were not affected by antibiotics. Then the focus of public health would move from infectious diseases to the diseases of aging such as cardiovascular diseases and cancer. Perhaps the most celebrated battle for a new vaccine was the one developed in the early 1950s to protect against polio.

The Saga of the March of Dimes and Doctor Salk Versus Polio

In 1921, Franklin Delano Roosevelt, who would later become president of the United States, contracted polio after swimming at his family estate on Campobello Island, just off the northern coast of Maine. Roosevelt was then 39 years old and was very active in politics for the Democratic Party. He had served as assistant secretary of the navy in the Wilson administration and had his eye on higher elected office. Most recently he had been the vice-presidential candidate on the Democratic ticket, which Governor William Cox of Ohio had headed — and lost — in the 1920 presidential election. Roosevelt's legs were paralyzed as a result of the polio, and for the rest of his life he would be able to move around only with the aid of a wheelchair. When the occasion demanded, he could walk several steps with his legs supported by heavy braces, crutches, and his iron determination.

This combination of events was to lead to the elimination of polio, usually a disease of children. When polio attacked the spinal cord (also attacking the muscle control necessary for normal breathing and respiration), it left its victims paralyzed to some extent about a third of the time. Polio was not a common disease at the time, but it was greatly feared by parents because children could be crippled before they really got started in life. Polio was caused by a virus, and until the 1950s there was no vaccine to prevent it. As a virus, antibiotics had no effect on it when they arrived in the 1930s and 1940s. There had been a relative epidemic of polio in 1916, the first time polio had caught widespread public notice in the United States.

Ironically, the outbreak of polio in the 1900s is felt to be due to the great advances in sanitation in the previous years. There is evidence of polio having been with mankind for a long time, but when there were plenty of open sewers and such, children routinely caught the disease in infancy when paralysis rarely occurs, and they were immune to it afterwards. When sanitation efforts removed this early contact, children and others were no longer immune to the episodes of polio that would randomly sweep through communities, most often in the summer. In a sense, public health caused the disease, but public health would ultimately eradicate it. The virus is apparently excreted in the stool, and then spread from hand to hand or hand to mouth by people, especially children, who wash their hands less often than they should. The ultimate entry point to the body is through the mouth.

When Roosevelt was afflicted, great pains were taken to get him up and around. Finally a deal, probably impossible to arrange today, was struck with the media to avoid taking pictures showing Roosevelt being transferred from train to automobile or from wheelchair to his desk when he appeared most helpless. Roosevelt developed immense upper-arm strength to be able to brace himself when standing so he could appear as normal as possible. He looked constantly for cures or exercise regimes that would help, and as part of this effort he bought a semi-resort in Warm Springs, Georgia, whose waters were thought to have curative effects.

The resort could not be turned into a paying proposition, and a close friend of Roosevelt, D. Basil O'Connor, who was essentially Roosevelt's personal lawyer and the head of a New York law firm that paid Roosevelt a salary mostly for attaching the Roosevelt name to the firm, was asked by Roosevelt to take over management of Warm Springs when it was clear that it could not be financially sustained. Roosevelt did not want to give it up as a source of some therapy, and it became a presidential retreat where Roosevelt could relax and appear as he was without anyone seeing. O'Connor, known to his friends as "Doc"—although he was a lawyer and certainly not a doctor — turned Warm Springs into a foundation that could accept donations. Warm Springs became the National Foundation for Infantile Paralysis, and it also became a fund-raising machine, especially with the publicity brought to it with Roosevelt as president.

The foundation did an immense amount of good, treating polio patients in Warm Springs and raising funds for crutches and wheelchairs and the so-called iron lungs that "breathed" for polio patients who could not breathe on their own. It supported polio-oriented hospitals and raised a lot of money to find a cure for the disease. At first funds were raised through a series of presidential birthday balls, glitzy social events held across the country near the president's birthday in January. But in 1938, Hollywood stars including comedian Eddie Cantor, who had been involved with the presidential galas, proposed using their radio programs to solicit funds on a broader basis. Playing on the name of the very popular newsreel feature known as the "March of Time," Cantor suggested using the name March of Dimes, where listeners would pledge at least one dime for the support of research into infantile paralysis and send it directly to the White House.

The promotion was an astounding success. The first appeal by Cantor was made during the last week of January 1938 to coincide with the presidential birthday balls still being held near the president's birthday. The Lone Ranger also made a similar appeal on his radio program. Two days after Cantor's program, the usual White House mail of 5,000 letters swelled to 30,000 with letters containing dimes. The next day 50,000 letters came in; the day after that, 150,000. The White House mail office hired 50 extra mail clerks, but they still couldn't cope with the onslaught. When the mail had cleared, the foundation had raised $1.8 million dollars, of which $268,000 had been sent a dime at a time. The March of Dimes would become the prime source of funding in the battle against polio, and the National Foundation for Infantile Paralysis would become the main source of research funds to fight the disease.

After World War II, it is possible that returning soldiers brought the polio virus back with them from places they had been that were below the sanitation levels of the United States. In any event, polio began to appear in the news on a regular basis. (The official name of the disease, poliomyelitis, was shortened to polio around this time to conserve headline space.) There were 25,000 cases of polio reported in 1946, and the number grew to 58,000 in 1952. An accelerated effort was being made to develop a vaccine to use against the disease, now known to be caused by a virus that affected only humans, monkeys, and chimpanzees. It was also suspected that although the virus had many strains, there were only three basic types. A vaccine against all three types in one combined dose was clearly feasible.

Dr. Jonas Salk, a young doctor interested in such research, had accepted a post at the University of Pittsburgh, which was not a place that ranked high on the prestige list, but one that promised a young doctor space and other facilities for research in order to attract doctors to Pittsburgh. Salk accepted a grant from the March of Dimes to work on a typing program to insure there were only three types of polio viruses. The program could be tedious, but it gave Salk the cash support he needed for his laboratory. A major breakthrough was made at the time when a researcher in bacteriology and immunology named John Enders discovered how to grow the polio virus in human tissue other than that from the nervous system (nervous system tissue could not be used to create a vaccine because much research had showed that any injections of nervous system tissue into a person caused fatal allergic brain damage). Before this, only monkeys could be used to support the research. And it was tedious to give monkeys the virus, wait for them to become ill, and then take the long series of steps necessary to ultimately develop a vaccine. The discovery by Enders greatly speeded up the research process, and Enders would share the Nobel Prize in 1954 for his work.

Salk took advantage of the breakthrough by Enders to rapidly complete his program of typing the virus, and since he was far ahead of other researchers in this area, he immediately moved ahead with work on a vaccine. His vaccine would use a killed virus to be sure there was no danger of giving a case of polio with the vaccination shot. General wisdom in the area said greatly weakened live virus should be used because it was felt it would provide immunity for a much longer time than a killed virus. But doctors favoring this course said it would take another 15 years or so to develop a safe and effective virus. With more children being crippled every day, Basil O'Connor, head of the March of Dimes, decided to further support Salk, whose initial test results were very promising. A dramatic political battle broke out when many doctors said Salk had overstepped his bounds with his initial tests, but O'Connor stood solidly behind Salk. O'Connor stated that Salk may or may not have developed the ideal vaccine, but he had developed a vaccine that appeared to work, and it was time to stop talking and act. Salk cited the old saying: "to await certainty is to await eternity."

In 1954, after much argument and discussion, Salk had a vaccine he was so sure would work he vaccinated his own three sons. On April 26, 1954, a carefully worked out test program, sponsored by the March of Dimes among much contention, began to vaccinate over 650,000 children across the nation with Salk's vaccine. When the vaccination program was over, 1.8 million children took part, though not all received the vaccine to insure a statistically accurate trial.

The following year, on April 12, 1955, the results of the test program were announced on the anniversary of President Roosevelt's death a decade earlier in 1945. The test program was an unqualified success. The terse first words of the press release said it all: "The vaccine works. It is safe, effective, and potent." Newspapers and radio and television broadcasts around the world carried the news. Jonas Salk was a hero. Later, a weakened live virus, the Sabin vaccine became available. It was much easier to administer than the Salk vaccine, requiring only the swallowing of a sugar cube, rather than the shots in the arm required by the Salk vaccine. But even today countries have disputes over which vaccine to use in their public health programs. There is no known record of paralytic polio being contacted from properly prepared Salk vaccine, but with almost statistical certainty a few cases occur from the Sabin vaccine because in a weakened live virus vaccine, some viruses still are potent enough to cause the disease. But in spite of this problem, cases of paralytic polio fell from 135 per million prior to the Salk vaccine to 26 per million after, and today they stand at 4 per million. This is a tragedy for the few who contract the disease from the vaccine, but on an overall public health basis, polio is no longer an infectious disease issue.

The triumph over polio marked the entrance of the federal government into public health issues in a big way, as is discussed later in this introduction. But it also marked the turning of the focus of public health from infectious diseases to the diseases of aging, like cardiovascular diseases and cancer. The next section, on the measurement of public health, shows how the main causes of death in the United States moved firmly into the diseases of aging. The section also discusses how the prime battle against infectious diseases as a major cause of death had been won even before antibiotics appeared on the scene.

Measuring the Degree of Success of Public Health Policies — A Primer on Life Expectancy and Death Rates

The best measurements for determining the success or failure of public health efforts are life expectancy and death rates. These measures are effectively one measure expressed in different terms. They show where the prime resources of public health efforts should be focused. But medical breakthroughs are required to determine the probable causes of these diseases so that public health programs like vaccination and education can be implemented to help prevent the spread and even the development, if possible, of these diseases. To understand these changes in focus of public health, it is necessary to understand life expectancies and death rates and how they are used as measures of public health.

The life expectancy of the people in a given nation is high as long as the death rates are low and vice versa. Life expectancy is a forecast of the expected average life of any person at a given age. Strictly speaking, the calculation of the remaining years of life is a life expectation because expectation is a mathematical term related to data derived using specific rules of probability. The calculation is made using life tables that make certain assumptions about future death rates at different ages. Differences in the assumptions and methods of calculation can provide different results.

Life expectancy can vary with the race of the group being measured, and in the early twentieth century in the United States good data are not available for all ages of all races. It is important to note that life expectancy is an average. A life expectancy of 70 years at birth means that 50 percent of the people born in that year will live to be 70 or more. A life expectancy of 15 years at age 70 means that 50 percent of the people who are 70 in that year will live to be 85 or more, i.e., at least another 15 years. A life expectancy of 5 years at age 85 means that 50 percent of the people who are 85 years old that year will live to be 90, i.e., another 5 years. Life expectancy is never zero. At all ages, a person has additional life expectancy. But detailed forecasts usually are not made much beyond 85 years of age.

Maximum life span is much different than life expectancy. Maximum life span is the oldest age attainable for a member of the species. For humans, the maximum life span is considered by most experts to be about 115 years. There have been many claims of people living longer than this, but acceptable documentation of their ages is lacking. The person who lived the longest with good documentation is a French woman who attained an age of about 123 years. Thus, for the billions of people alive today, 115 years remains a likely maximum, and very few people will actually achieve an age anywhere near that.

The maximum age any person has managed to achieve has little relevance to individual life expectancy. The maximum life span for humans probably has not changed by any meaningful amount for centuries. Human life expectancy has not increased as a result of an increasing maximum life span. Life expectancy has increased because a greater number of people live longer after birth than they previously managed to do. Life expectancy at any age essentially adds the total number of years that probably will be lived by the group being measured and then divides by the number of people in the group. As more people live longer, the average length of life increases, and thus life expectancy increases. Life expectancy at birth is strongly dependent on the number of deaths occurring relatively early in life, because people dying early lose a high number of years of probable life. As such early deaths decline, life expectancy at birth increases substantially.

For example, life expectancy at birth in the United States increased by 60 percent for white males (from just under 47 years to just under 75 years) and 63 percent for women (from just under 49 years to 80 years) between

1900 and 2000. This reflects substantially reduced death rates from infectious diseases in the earlier years of life. Life expectancy at other ages than birth also increased but by smaller percentages. This is because the number of years lived by an average person increases by smaller and smaller amounts as the maximum average life span is approached.

For example, life expectancy at age 85 increased only by 1.8 percent for men and 2.9 percent for women between 1900 and 2000. For both men and women today, life expectancy at age 85 is forecasted to increase by only about 0.1 years every five years. This indicates that the average maximum life expectancy is close to 85. This means life expectancy at birth would not be expected to increase much beyond 85, although women have a somewhat higher limit and will arrive at their limit sooner than men. This makes age 85 a reasonable goal for men and women at any age, and it suggests that premature death could be defined as death before the age of 85.

The substantial increases in life expectancy obtained during the last century are almost entirely due to public health achievements. Deaths from infectious diseases fell dramatically during the century, and nearly this entire decline was achieved before the advent of antibiotic drugs in the late 1930s and early 1940s. Because of improvements in public health due to improved sanitation and vaccination programs, the death rate in the United States has declined substantially, with the biggest declines coming before 1940. If death rates continue to change favorably with time, life expectancies will continue to increase, as was the experience during the entire twentieth century. However, the improvements came in smaller and smaller increments as the century progressed.

By far the highest death rates for a single cause in any year in the twentieth century were the 588.5 deaths per 100,000 due to pneumonia/flu in 1918, during the great global flu epidemic. The next highest rate was the 375.2 level produced by heart disease in 1963. But while the 32.5 percent of all deaths caused by pneumonia/flu in 1918 was an extremely high level for the time, the 39 percent of all deaths caused by heart disease in 1963 was similar to the average percentage for heart disease from 1950 through the 1980s. The significant difference in the impact of the percentage of deaths was due to the much lower total death rate in the later years as compared to that of 1918. The total death rate declined because deaths from infectious disease fell much faster than the increase in deaths due to cardiovascular diseases and cancer in the later decades.

The need to consider both death rates and percentage of deaths is demonstrated best by the changes in each for cardiovascular disease and cancer from 1900 through 2000. The death rate due to cardiovascular disease in 2000 was around 330, while in 1900 it was about 345. Thus, the cardiovascular disease death rate actually fell during the century (a surprise to many, but it must be noted that heart disease is just one part of cardiovascular disease). However, the percentage of deaths caused by cardiovascular diseases in 2000 was close to 40 percent compared to 20 percent in 1900. Thus, the percentage of deaths due to cardiovascular disease essentially doubled between 1900 and 2000 even though the absolute death rate declined. This was because the total death rate from all causes in 2000 was about 850 compared to 1,719 in 1900, a decrease during the century of almost half.

As far as cancer is concerned, the death rate increased from 64 per 100,000 in 1900 to about 195 in 2000. But because, as noted, the total death rate dropped so dramatically between 1900 and 2000, the percentage of deaths caused by cancer increased from less than 4 percent in 1900 to over 23 percent in 2000. This is an increase of about 6:1. This means that while the combined death rate for cardiovascular diseases and cancer increased from just over 400 in 1900 to about 530 in 2000, the percentage of deaths caused by the two diseases increased from 24 percent in 1900 to over 60 percent in 2000. It's the 60 percent figure that grabs our attention today.

In summary, the overall performance of public health in the United States in the twentieth century is extremely good. The overall death rate in the country has fallen by approximately half. However, the mix of diseases making up the death rate has also changed dramatically. If we focus only on the percentage of deaths caused by a particular disease, instead of on the reduction in the total death rate, we will miss the substantial improvements made in public health. But it is important to know what diseases currently account for the largest percentages of death so that we can point public health in the proper directions. For example, around 1900 there was little educational material available pointing out the dangers of smoking, but lots of material discussed how to avoid infectious diseases. In today's world, there is relatively little information about infectious diseases other than the need to have our children properly vaccinated at the proper times (AIDS is an infectious disease that does get a lot of publicity, although it accounts for less than 1 percent of all deaths and does not even make the top ten list), but there is voluminous material about the dangers of smoking. We try to accurately measure the overall impact of public health by studying death rates over time, but we need to focus on the percentages of deaths caused by certain diseases in order to know where to apply our public health resources.

While we are discussing death rates and causes of death due to certain diseases, we need to understand that the causes of death noted on a death certificate have changed during the century. These changes are determined by international conferences, and the changes were necessary as the understanding of disease processes improved. However, such changes produce obvious difficulties in determining consistent results over time. This is separate from the fact that when an elderly person with multiple diseases dies, it is not always easy to tell exactly which disease caused the death.

For example, for many years bronchitis, emphysema, asthma, and other related diseases were shown as separate entries from diseases included in a broad category of "all other." Since 1980, these diseases have been grouped together as "chronic obstructive pulmonary diseases and allied conditions" or COPD. This is an important category as the population ages, because these diseases are fatal primarily in older persons. But before 1980, there was no such identified disease as COPD, even if the underlying diseases did exist.

This kind of change is further complicated by the hundreds of different codes used to identify specific diseases as causes of death. Because these codes often identify different sites of diseases, rather than a substantially different cause of disease, large groupings of diseases are made that bring the total down to a manageable number. This concept of disease by site is useful in helping to understand certain key causes of death.

For example, "infectious diseases" is a term that includes hundreds of diseases with different causes. But the prime causes can be grouped into the broad categories of bacteria, virus, and parasites (such as worms). Treatments vary widely, but drugs are the main line of attack against bacteria and parasites, while vaccination is the key defense against viruses. The common factor of these diseases is that they are caused by an outside invader affecting the body. If we consider them by site, we can group them in an intelligent way that makes it easy to understand their rise and fall (and possible rise again) during the last century and into this century.

COPD, as discussed above, is an attempt to group different diseases affecting one basic site: the respiratory system. Pneumonia/flu and tuberculosis are also primarily diseases of the respiratory system, but they are listed separately because they were such big killers early in the twentieth century (pneumonia/flu is still an important factor today, due to the aging of the population). Continuing by site, gastritis has been used in many death certificates to include diseases of the digestive tract such as diarrhea, enteritis, duodenitis, and colitis. However, all of these diseases have fallen to such low levels that even the word "gastritis" as an overall cumulative term no longer appears separately as a cause of death.

The category "other infectious diseases" usually includes diseases such as diphtheria, typhoid, whooping cough, measles, scarlet fever, and streptococcal sore throat. At one time all of these were major killers but, as has happened with gastritis, many occur now so infrequently as to be statistically insignificant. AIDS is an example of another infectious disease that has become a large enough killer to be listed separately (even though it presently accounts only for less than 1 percent of all deaths in the United States).

If the term "infectious diseases" is defined to include all the diseases listed above, we can say there are (and have been) only four basic causes of death in the United States in the twentieth century. The first category is cardiovascular disease (heart disease, stroke, and related problems), which has been the primary killer since 1920 and was a major killer even in the years before. The second category is cancer, which now ranks only behind cardiovascular disease, a position it has held since 1940 (as noted, cardiovascular disease and cancer now account for almost two-thirds of all deaths). The third major cause is infectious diseases. They were the leading killer before 1920, due to pneumonia/flu and tuberculosis, but now combined account for only about 10 percent of all deaths. The fourth category is violent deaths, which includes accidents, suicide, and homicide. This fourth category causes about 6 percent of all deaths.

These four groups now account for a little over 80 percent of all deaths, and they accounted for about 75 percent in 1900. Thus, the total number of deaths caused by just these four groups changed very little during the twentieth century. But as emphasized before, the relative importance of each category has changed dramatically. This change is primarily due to the efforts of public health. Infectious deaths of all sorts have been substantially reduced, and the key efforts of public health now focus on trying to educate people about the chronic diseases of the cardiovascular system and cancer. But contrary to the thoughts of many people, our present chronic diseases of the cardiovascular system have been a key factor in deaths at every point in the twentieth century. Essentially the key change over the years is that infectious diseases have been replaced by cancer as the prime killer after cardiovascular disease. It must be emphasized that this analysis of public health applies only to the United States and similar nations. In much of the world, infectious diseases are still big killers, and people do not live long enough to deal with the diseases of aging.

A final important concept to understand when discussing death rates is the concept of age-adjusted death rates. Death rates as generally discussed are determined by dividing the number of deaths by the number of people to get a rate per 100,000. But as the population ages, one could argue death rates are overstated, because a higher rate would be expected for an older population. In the United States, age-adjusted death rates are determined by selecting a population baseline such as 1940 (which is used by the U.S. Census Bureau in its *Statistical Abstract of the United States* and the American Heart Association). Present death rates for specific age brackets are applied to the age brackets of the population as it existed in 1940. This eliminates age differences over time when determining whether deaths due to a specific disease are increasing or decreasing, and at what rate. At appropriate points to come, we will discuss age-adjusted death rates versus raw death rates when discussing the effects of public health on certain chronic diseases.

All the data we have discussed so far relative to life expectancies and death rates applies only to the United States since 1900. The calculation of life expectancies and death rates in other countries actually started about 200 years before 1900. Edmund Halley, the man after whom Halley's Comet is named, published one of the first tables of life expectancies in 1693. He analyzed records from the city of Breslau and found a life expectancy at birth of 33 years and a life expectancy at age 80 of 6 years. Over 300 years later, life expectancy at birth in the United States for all races was just under 77, a gain of 44 years. But life expectancy at age 80 was less than 9 years, a gain of only 3 years in three centuries.

This is another example showing that although life expectancy at birth has continually increased, life expectancy after age 80 has changed relatively little. This is because increasing life expectancy at birth is due to the reduction of premature death (i.e., death before age 85). Once a person passes 80, there is little premature death to prevent. If the maximum life span does not change much over time, life expectancy at advanced ages will change very little. This is precisely what has happened since records have been kept, confirming that the maximum life span has not changed.

It is estimated that life expectancy at birth in Europe was 18 or less for many centuries after humans appeared on the scene (remember life expectancy is essentially an average which half the people exceed and half do not). By the time of the Roman Empire, about 2,000 years ago, life expectancy had climbed to about 22 years. In the Middle Ages it was over 30 years, and it grew to about 35 years by the time the Revolutionary War started in the United States. Over the next 125 years, life expectancy at birth in the United States increased to the high 40s, reaching a level of about 47 years by 1900. In a broad sense, all of these improvements were due to improvements in public health, even if the people in charge did not know why their recommended changes were advantageous. Sanitarians of each era get most of the credit for that improvement. With the coming of the germ theory of disease in the late 1800s, the improvements in life expectancy in just the twentieth century were as great as those made in the previous several centuries.

An Overview of Death by Decade in the United States

The effectiveness of public health initiatives in the United States in the twentieth century is best shown by the changes in selected death rates over time. Using age-adjusted data for a moment to permit good comparisons over the century, the male death rate in the United States in 1900 was just over 18 deaths per 1,000 people, and the female death rate was just under 17 deaths per 1,000 people. The male death rate was higher at every point in the century, but it had fallen to an age-adjusted level of just over 6 deaths per 1,000 by the year 2000, a reduction of about 70 percent. The female death rate fell to just under 4 deaths per 1,000 by the year 2000, a reduction of about 80 percent.

The reduction in the death rate was relatively smooth during the century, although the improvements early on were due mainly to reductions in deaths from infectious disease. The continuing improvements near the end of the century were due to reductions in deaths due to cardiovascular disease (heart disease, strokes, and related problems), somewhat offset by a continual increase in cancer deaths. These increased cancer deaths were due to both males and females taking up smoking at increased rates near the middle of the century. The rate of reduction in total death rates has leveled off since the 1980s, but they would have continued to fall more sharply if people had never begun to smoke. The greatest focus of public health education today is getting people to stop smoking and getting teenagers and young adults not to begin smoking.

Incidentally, the person with the smallest probability of dying at a given age is an 11-year-old female. It has been shown before that the immune system seems to peak around this period, and then loses efficacy slowly for the rest of the person's life. Also, an 11-year-old female is past all of the many problems that young children have in their first several years of life but has not yet entered upon new problems that occur in the adolescent and adult years.

The change in the basic causes of death during the century are best shown by sampling raw death rate data for causes of death at different points in the century. In 1900, pneumonia/flu, tuberculosis, and "other infectious diseases" shared the top of the death rate list. Pneumonia/flu caused almost 12 percent of all deaths; tuberculosis just over 11 percent; and "other infectious diseases" just under 11 percent. If one includes gastritis, the fourth most prevalent cause of death in 1900, the four leading causes of death — all infectious diseases — accounted for just over 42 percent of all deaths. The fifth and sixth causes were heart disease and stroke, and if one lumps these two diseases together with other cardiovascular problems into a category called "cardiovascular diseases," they account for just over 20 percent of all deaths. The ten leading categories of death accounted for about 80 percent of all deaths, while cancer, in ninth place, caused just fewer than 4 percent of all deaths.

By 1910, heart disease as a single cause took over the top place in the causes-of-death list, and except for the pneumonia/flu epidemic of 1918, heart disease remains the highest single leading cause of death today. This is a different result than many people expect, because it has often been said that heart disease is caused by the frenzied and complicated lifestyles we

developed as the century progressed. However, heart disease has been a leading killer for nearly a full century. In 1918, a pneumonia/flu epidemic caused
nearly 33 percent of all deaths and racked up the highest death rate for a
single cause in any time in the century. However, as the 1920s got underway,
heart disease quickly moved back into first place.

By 1940, just before the wide application of the sulfa drugs and penicillin, both considered miracle drugs that wiped out many virulent bacteria,
heart disease and other cardiovascular problems including stroke accounted
for over 45 percent of all deaths. Cancer was the second-ranked cause of
death, producing just over 11 percent of all deaths. Thus, cardiovascular diseases and cancer accounted for 56 percent of all deaths. The leading cause
of death behind these broad categories was the 7 percent caused by accidents.
Pneumonia/flu, other infectious diseases, and tuberculosis deaths only accounted
for 16 percent of all deaths, with pneumonia/flu being the leading single
infectious cause at less than 7 percent. Thus, it must be noted again that long
before antibiotics came on the scene, deaths due to infectious diseases had
fallen from over 42 percent in 1900 to 16 percent in 1940. This was primarily
the result of improved public health measures, ranging from sanitary initiatives to vaccinations.

By 1960, heart disease as a single cause of death produced almost 39
percent of all deaths and had a death rate of 369 per 100,000 compared to the
previously incredible death rate of 589 per 100,000 due to pneumonia/flu
during the great flu epidemic of 1918. Some doctors even used the word epidemic to define the sharp rise in deaths due to heart attacks in the 1960s.
But better treatment and much better education about cardiovascular diseases brought about by the public health movement have driven deaths due
to heart disease downward ever since. By the end of the century, the heart
disease death rate was down to about 258, and heart disease caused about
30 percent of all deaths. This is really a dramatic result when one realizes
that heart disease primarily affects elderly people, and the elderly population is continuing to grow substantially in the United States. Together with
great improvements in treatment, public health efforts to teach people the
proper lifestyles to avoid cardiovascular problems have been very effective.

In an effort to bring to the attention of the public how important
lifestyle factors are in avoiding premature death, in 2000 the U.S. Public
Health Service (PHS) showed death rates as a function of lifestyle factors.
For example, where cardiovascular diseases including heart disease and stroke
and related factors accounted for about 38 percent of all deaths, with another
23 percent being caused by cancer, the PHS showed the actual causes of death
in the United States in a terminology many people were not familiar with.
The PHS estimated that tobacco accounted for 18 percent of all deaths, poor
diet and physical inactivity accounted for almost 17 percent, and alcohol con-

sumption accounted for 3.5 percent. These three causes, all of which are essentially lifestyle choices, far outweighed any other specific causes of death such as infectious diseases (3 percent), toxic agents (2.3 percent), motor vehicle accidents (1.8 percent), firearms (1.2 percent), and so forth. Even such well-publicized lifestyle choices as unsafe sexual behavior (0.8 percent) and illicit drug use (0.7 percent) were relatively tiny causes of death, even though they might bring great pain to certain individuals.

Probably the disease most feared by individuals is cancer. So despite great strides in reducing cardiovascular diseases, the PHS has tried to educate the public as well as make new advances in treatment. Cancer death rates have more than tripled between 1900 and 2000. They have increased at a steady rate, but it is misleading to look at cancer as an individual disease. There are actually a number of different cancers, all of which differ by the particular site in the body they attack. This is one reason why the so-called war on cancer has had limited success. It is analogous to the fact that flu, or the common cold, is essentially incurable, because it is not one disease, but many. The flu virus continues to change as it moves between the human race and animals, and thus one vaccine cannot be developed to protect against all forms of the virus. In a similar way, every type of cancer is unique to the site in which it arises. And it continues to have this nature, wherever it metastasizes. For example, prostate cancer often spreads to the bone, but the characteristics of the metastasized cancer is like that of prostate cancer, not like that of bone cancer, which is a separate disease.

Generally speaking, there is a cure for cancer in the sense that if it is found before it metastasizes, it can be cut out surgically. However, cancer cannot be surgically removed from all sites. Thus, cancer continues to be an intractable problem. People probably fear it primarily because when they are told they have cancer, they feel they have been given a death sentence. They know specifically they're going to die, rather than just knowing it in the general sense in that everybody eventually dies. But cancer can be attacked by specific lifestyle changes that affect the origin of cancer in given sites.

For example, in men lung cancer has become by far the biggest killer among all cancers. In 1930 the biggest killer of men was stomach cancer, followed by colorectal cancer, prostate cancer, and lung cancer. In 1950, the death rate from these four cancers was essentially equal. The number of cases of lung cancer increased and the cases of stomach cancer fell. Stomach cancer in both men and women has constantly fallen due, it is assumed, to improvements in food processing and the elimination of certain irritants from certain foods. Since 1950, colorectal cancer and prostate cancer have been essentially constant at the same rate with prostate cancer moving slightly ahead of colorectal cancer as the century ended, probably because there are so many new techniques to detect prostate cancer. But lung cancer has climbed dramatically. Since the 1940s, lung cancer has increased by a factor of seven, all due to the use of tobacco. Prostate and colorectal cancer are stable and are the cause of death at a rate of about one third of that of lung cancer. Stomach cancer, in the meantime, the biggest killer in the 1930s, has fallen by a factor of nearly six times and is now a minor issue. Thus, cancer in men — except for lung cancer — has been declining since the 1930s. If men had never taken up smoking, their cancer rate would have fallen dramatically since the 1930s. And smoking is certainly a lifestyle choice.

For women, the big cancer killers in 1930, in order, were uterine cancer, breast cancer, and colorectal cancer. These cancers had roughly equal rates, while lung cancer in the 1930s trailed the other three by a factor of 10. The development of the Pap test cut uterine cancer rates by 1950, and uterine cancer was only in third place then behind colorectal and breast cancer, both of which continued at an equal pace. Lung cancer had crept up to be about a fifth of the other rates. By the end of the twentieth century, uterine cancer had become a minor cancer killer, with a rate that was only about a third of that of colorectal cancer. Breast cancer, contrary to common knowledge, was at nearly the same rate as it had been in 1930. In fact, breast cancer peaked in 1940, and it has maintained nearly the same death rate level for over 70 years, even though it is the second leading killer of women. However, the death rate for women from lung cancer soared past that for breast cancer somewhere in the mid–1980s, and it has continued to be the greatest killer of women ever since. Lung cancer in women follows closely the same growth curve as it does in men, except that it is offset by about 20 years, reflecting the delay in the time at which women took up smoking at the same rate as men. The prime difference today is that the lung cancer rate in men has begun to plateau, while in women it is still growing.

Thus, cancer statistics can be very misleading. If considered by site, with lung cancer out of the picture for the moment, total cancer rates for both men and women have fallen steadily since the 1930s. However, lung cancer has grown dramatically, and therefore cancer in total has also grown dramatically. If men and women would cease smoking, the death rates due to cancer in the future would continue to fall.

There is a great deal of litigation today being brought by both government entities and individuals against companies that manufacture smoking products. Government entities want to recover their prior costs of caring for persons made ill by smoking. Generally they have been successful in winning multi-billion dollar awards. Often the money awarded is used for other purposes than those that are strictly related to smoking issues, but most government entities are commonly hard pressed for revenues, and tobacco companies are a relatively easy target in today's world. Thus, such litigation seems sure to continue.

Individuals generally claim they were tricked by tobacco company advertising into becoming addicted to smoking before they could fully appreciate its now-widely-known dangers. Some juries rule in their favor, and others do not, citing the concept of personal responsibility for choosing to smoke. This kind of litigation will probably continue as long as tobacco companies can continue to pay the damages that are awarded.

Some analysts note that doctors, who have seen first hand the ugly results of smoking, have been able to quit smoking nearly completely, however addictive the habit may be. Perhaps doctors have greater motivation to quit because of what they have seen. Since the advent of the surgeon general's report on smoking in 1964 (an excellent example of the educational efforts of the Public Health Service), many Americans overall have stopped smoking. When the report came out, 42 percent of American adults smoked. But 30 years later, that level decreased to about 25 percent. Doctors as a group have shown much more substantial reductions. In 1960 it was estimated that a whopping 79 percent of all doctors smoked. However, by 1995 just over three percent of doctors were still smoking. Considering the reduction from 79 percent smokers to only 3 percent, it can be concluded that essentially 96 percent of all smoking doctors have been able to quit. It certainly seems true that the key factor helping doctors avoid this addiction is the high degree of motivation they get from seeing the tragic results of smoking every day.

The issue of smoking is another area in which the public health of the United States differs greatly from the rest of the world in a favorable way. Countless restaurants, bars, and other such public places in the United States have banned smoking. Nearly all governmental buildings and many corporate buildings do not permit smoking. All forms of public transportation including airlines and trains and buses ban smoking. The issue of second-hand smoke has eliminated the right of anyone to smoke anywhere. This demonstrates that substantial changes can be made nationally in the name of public health once the relevant facts are widely understood. In many other countries smoking is still pervasive. It is sales to these other countries that enable the tobacco companies to pay the damage awards described above.

It is notable that even though the dangers of smoking are numerous, the 17 percent of deaths caused by poor diet/physical inactivity is almost equal to the 18 percent caused by tobacco. In order to help the public understand this problem, public health officials have adopted a measurement called body mass index, used in place of the height/weight tables that had been used for decades. One problem with the weight tables, the most common of which were issued by the Metropolitan Life Insurance Company starting in 1943, is that doctors and insurance salesmen, among others, have lobbied to make the tables more lenient. The irony is that the tables were originally published to show the experience of the insurance company with its policyholders. When an insurance company, which anxiously wants to keep you alive and relieve them from needing to pay out death benefits early, recommends ways to live longer, you can be sure its advice is objective. But the tables unfortunately moved from a table of weight levels most likely to avoid early deaths to a table of desirable weights to a table of typical weights. This finally becomes an exercise in making people feel they are not too far overweight.

Because there were other problems with the basic height/weight tables for persons who were very muscular and thus seemed too heavy for their height, and because people in the United States grew steadily taller and heavier over the years, the body mass index was developed to set a wider range of standards to determine both underweight and overweight people in medical terms. If studied carefully, the body mass index (BMI) gives desirable weights for heights that are very close to the originally recommended weight and height tables that were issued by the Metropolitan Insurance Company back in the 1940s.

The *Third National Health and Nutrition Examination Survey, 1988–1994* found 59 percent of men and 49 percent of women with BMIs over 25, which is considered overweight. Extreme obesity (a BMI over 40), a condition demanding immediate medical care, was found in 2 percent of the men and 4 percent of the women. Other surveys since 1994 show a steadily worsening condition (a recent survey found two-thirds of Americans to be overweight with half of those entering at least the first level of obesity). Few things are more popular — or more contentious — than special diet plans. Most people are unwilling to accept that the best way to lose weight is to eat less and exercise more. Public health educational programs attempt to stress this fact, but it is a tough sell. People understandably like to eat and drink, and the expectation of a possible few more years of life in the dim future is a small incentive for many. But the prime incentive is to avoid a lowered quality of life when one gets older — which everyone alive does — and living at a lowered quality level can go on for a long time.

Public Health Organization in the United States

The individual states and cities carried most of the burden of organizing to carry out public health initiatives before 1900. The federal government became generally more involved in the twentieth century, and after 1950 the federal government took over by far the leading role. A key public health department of the federal government is the Food and Drug Administration (FDA), and its evolution traces the chronology of much of the federal government's actions in public health.

The Food and Drug Administration (FDA) now oversees areas accounting for about 25 percent of the total dollars spent by consumers. It is a combined regulatory, scientific, and public health education agency that oversees most food products (except meat and poultry), drugs (for both humans and animals), therapeutic agents of biological origin (like vaccines), medical devices (including those that produce radiation), cosmetics, and animal feed. Many key parts of our lives and activities are monitored by the FDA.

The United States was an agricultural country at its beginning, and the government supported the efforts of farmers through the Department of Agriculture. The FDA grew from a single chemist in the Department of Agriculture in 1862, supporting efforts to screen mainly imports for impure or adulterated food or drugs. This effort grew to cover the whole country internally because individual state laws were very inconsistent. The FDA grew to an agency with a staff of over 9,000 people and a budget of $1.3 billion in 2001. The FDA entered its era of key growth in 1906 with the passage of the Federal Food and Drug Act. The agency assumed its present name in 1930. The FDA was part of the Department of Agriculture until 1940, when it became part of the new Federal Security Agency. In 1953, when the Salk vaccine was beginning to appear on the horizon, the FDA became part of the newly formed Health, Education, and Welfare (HEW) department. In 1968, the FDA became part of the Public Health Service within HEW, and in 1980 when public education became a separate department, HEW became the Department of Health and Human Services, and the FDA remained there, as it has ever since.

The folk hero of the FDA was Harvey Washington Wiley, who arrived as chief chemist in 1883. Wiley expanded the division's research in the area of the adulteration and misbranding of foods and drugs and helped spur public indignation about the problem by publishing "Foods and Food Adulterants" from 1887 to 1902. Wiley conducted highly publicized poison squad experiments in which volunteers consumed varying amounts of questionable food additives to determine the impact of additives on health. Wiley unified various groups to support laws against food adulteration, including state chemists and food and drug inspectors, the General Federation of Women's Clubs, and national associations of physicians and pharmacists. Wiley demonstrated that much more could be accomplished in the area of public health when grassroots support existed.

Sometimes people confuse the FDA with RDA, but the RDA (recommended dietary allowance) is an output of the Food and Nutrition Board of the National Academy of Sciences. They set the recommended daily input of various nutrients based on ongoing human and animal research. The board has met roughly every five years and has coordinated its research with Canada and some other foreign countries. The RDA is becoming the dietary reference intake or DRI. Many people previously referred to the RDA as the recommended daily allowance, but the confusion is irrelevant. The RDA has been a recommend standard of daily food intakes for many years and is used widely as an acceptable reference for planning meals.

The United States Public Health Service (PHS) was created in 1798 by an act of congress signed by President John Adams to provide relief for sick and disabled merchant seamen (Adams was a great supporter of the navy and merchant ships of all sorts). Known as the Marine Hospital Service, the PHS evolved into also performing purely public health services such as the quarantine and medical inspection of immigrants in the late nineteenth century. Accordingly, the name of the service was changed to the Public Health and Marine Hospital Service in 1902. The name was changed again in 1912 to the Public Health Service (PHS) to reflect the directing of the activities of the service towards public health activities. The Treasury Department was home to the PHS until 1939, when the Federal Security Agency was created to combine some health- and welfare-oriented activities, mainly the FDA and the PHS, as well as Social Security and Education. As noted in the FDA chronology, this evolved into the Department of Health and Human Services in 1980.

The PHS consists of the Office of Public Health and Science, ten regional health administrators, and eight operating divisions. These divisions include the FDA, as noted above; the Agency for Healthcare Research and Quality (AHRQ); the Agency for Toxic Substances and Disease Registry (ATSDR); the Centers for Disease Control and Prevention (CDC); Health Resources and Services Administration (HRSA); Indian Health Services (IHS); National Institutes of Health (NIH); and Substance Abuse and Mental Health Services Administration (SAMHSA). Other than the FDA, the best known divisions are probably the Centers for Disease Control, which are often involved in the analysis of exotic diseases such as Ebola, and the NIH, which support a wide-ranging number of programs for research into many diseases and disease processes.

The head of the PHS is the surgeon general of the United States, not to be confused with the surgeon generals of each of the armed forces. However, the surgeon general of the PHS does wear a uniform because technically the PHS is a commissioned corps tracing back to 1798 (the PHS can be militarized by the president in times of emergency). Essentially the PHS is run by the many professional personnel within its organization. The surgeon general mainly uses the service as a bully pulpit to focus national attention on various health issues.

The PHS now focuses primarily on the diseases of aging which are by far the prime causes of death in the United States. However, the service is a vast organization, and considerable work is being done on both old and new infectious diseases and the development of drugs and vaccines to combat them. In a world where an infectious disease in one part of the earth can be carried to another part within hours, either innocently via a airline passenger or with intended malice by a terrorist, the PHS has to be aware of diseases and disease processes everywhere, regardless of whether they presently appear in a significant way in the complex of diseases affecting residents of the United States.

AIDS is an example of a disease that is killing millions of persons outside the United States and is the leading cause of death in some countries. AIDS is caused by the Human Immunodeficiency Virus (HIV) that is believed to have originated in Africa in the late 1940s or early 1950s, with the first known case occurring in the Belgian Congo in 1959. The HIV virus is believed to have originated as a similar virus in monkeys, the blood of which was consumed in some way by humans. Some of the early cases in the United States were linked to a single flight attendant who is thought to have infected a large number of his thousands of sexual partners as he flew around the world (including Africa).

AIDS kills by essentially attacking the immune system and making its victim susceptible to a number of diseases, including specific kinds of cancer and pneumonia. As a virus, HIV is not susceptible to antibiotics, and no vaccine has been developed because the virus can, and does, readily change forms. But to spread AIDS requires intimate contact, like sexual intercourse, or acts where bodily fluids are directly interchanged, like injecting drugs with a tainted needle. Thus, it is actually very difficult to get AIDS today without practicing unsafe sex or injecting drugs. Some pharmaceutical drug cocktails have been developed that extend the life of AIDS victims, but educational programs telling people how to avoid getting AIDS have helped to keep its incidence statistically low in the United States. AIDS only accounts for less than 1 percent of the yearly deaths in the United States, but in countries with reduced resources and much lower educational levels where the first line of defense is likely to be a witch doctor, AIDS is wiping out generations of people (and driving life expectancies back into the 30s of years).

Other diseases like SARS, West Nile Virus, hantavirus, and the Marburg and Ebola viruses create headlines, but they have had no statistical impact on the United States. The PHS tracks these diseases and keeps an eye out for new diseases that may be unearthed as mankind continues to expand into the world's jungles and rain forests, where new diseases seem certain to lurk. But the main emphasis of the PHS today has to continue to be on the prosaic diseases like cancer and cardiovascular disease. And continual progress is being made every day on the prevention and treatment of these diseases in the United States.

THE CHRONOLOGY

As discussed in the introduction, the chronology of effective public health in the United States (and the rest of the world) really began with the injection for smallpox given by Dr. Edward Jenner in England in 1796. Many other actions intended to improve public health primarily via better sanitation and clean water supplies took place around the world before 1796, but Jenner's action marked the first that had a true scientific basis and hypothesis, and it was one that led to the savings of millions of lives in the centuries to come.

May 14, 1796—Dr. Edward Jenner injected material from a cowpox sore on the hand of a dairymaid named Sarah Nelmes into the arm of an eight-year-old boy named James Phipps. If Jenner's hypothesis was correct, this inoculation would cause the mild disease of cowpox, which would protect the boy from the dreaded disease of smallpox. Jenner later called this step a vaccination in honor of the Latin word for cow [vacca], because the cow was indirectly performing a noble service (the cow's hide was eventually preserved and now hangs in a museum). On July 1, 1796, Jenner, having noted that the boy had, as expected, developed and easily recovered from a case of cowpox, took the crucial step of next inoculating the boy with pus taken from a man with an active case of smallpox. As Jenner had hoped, the boy showed no reaction and never developed a case of smallpox. In years to come, Jenner would inoculate the boy with smallpox material 20 times, just to be sure he remained immune to smallpox. The boy never did catch smallpox, and Jenner had produced a revolution in medicine. He was so grateful to the boy, who was the son of day laborers who occasionally worked for Jenner, that Jenner built a cottage for the boy near his own house. Today that cottage is the Jenner Museum.

July 16, 1798— President John Adams signed an act of congress creating the U.S. Public Health Service. Adams was a fervent believer in a strong navy as well as a strong merchant fleet. The initial purpose of the Public Health Service (PHS) was to relieve sick and disabled seamen. The PHS was initially known as the Marine Hospital Service, and as the next century evolved, it would eventually begin to take on more public responsibilities including the quarantine and medical inspection of immigrants.

March 2, 1799— The Public Health Act of July 16, 1798, was amended on this date to extend the benefits of the Marine Hospital Service to officers and men of the United States Navy.

March 12, 1799— Dr. Benjamin Waterhouse of Harvard wrote an article about what he had read of Jenner's work and the miracle of cowpox preventing one from catching the dreaded smallpox. He followed this with a pamphlet titled *A Prospect of Extinguishing the Small-Pox* to encourage Jenner's technique to be used right away in the United States. He sent a copy of the pamphlet to John Adams, then president of the United States. He received a carefully worded answer that said in essence "don't call us, we'll call you." Waterhouse continued to experiment with the Jenner technique, and he vaccinated his five-year-old son in July of 1800. Waterhouse went on to vaccinate three more of his children and gained some notice in the local press.

April 5, 1800— As a good example of the type of problems that public health supporters had to deal with in the early days of the United States, the *Pittsburgh Gazette* reported that an ordinance had been passed that decreed that no one was to slaughter any animals (usually hogs) within the public market, or "lay any garbage, dung, or offal" therein. Large animals, including horses, roamed at will within many cities, and their manure and dead bodies littered many (dirt) streets. It is no wonder many sanitarians focused on these problems as sources of disease as the nineteenth century progressed.

December 1, 1800— Four months before the inauguration of the newly elected third president, Thomas Jefferson, Dr. Waterhouse sent to Jefferson another copy of the pamphlet on cowpox and smallpox that he had sent to John Adams in 1799. Jefferson, still officially the vice president, responded to Waterhouse on Christmas Day from Jefferson's estate in Monticello, Virginia. Jefferson was enthusiastic, noting he had read about Waterhouse's exploits in the newspaper, and Jefferson eventually asked for some material with which to perform vaccinations at Monticello. (Jefferson had gone through the dangerous so-called inoculation process when he was 23 and was himself immune to smallpox.)

January 1801—The Philadelphia water supply system, designed by Benjamin Latrobe, begin operation in this month. The system included an aqueduct and a distribution system of wooden pipes through which water was pumped by a steam engine. Frederick Graff was appointed engineer in 1805, and Graff served for 42 years, during which time he was acknowledge as the leading water system expert in the United States.

Philadelphia was just one of many cities to improve water supplies in this period. The major impetus for better water was the fear of yellow fever, which we know now is caused by mosquitoes and not a poor water supply per se, but this is just another example of good things being done in the name of sanitation even though the sanitarians were usually completely wrong about the basic cause of specific diseases.

November 1801—President Jefferson wrote a letter to a Doctor John Vaughn, describing how Jefferson had vaccinated about 200 persons at Monticello, including his family, his sons-in-law and their families, and neighbors who wished to take part. Jefferson had also written to Edward Jenner during 1801, congratulating him on his work. Jefferson's support of the vaccination process helped it get off to a good start as a standard practice in the United States, although there were many problems to overcome involving the purity of the vaccine before the Food and Drug Administration got well established as the twentieth century began.

May 3, 1802—On this date authorization was given to permit foreign seamen to use the services of the marine hospitals designated under the Public Health Act of July 16, 1798. The popular services could be used only on a reimbursable basis.

May 3, 1803—The first permanent hospital to be built specifically for the Marine Hospital Service was authorized on this date. The hospital was built in Boston, Massachusetts.

November 27, 1807—Dr. Benjamin Waterhouse, of local smallpox vaccination fame (*see entry for* March 12, 1799), was appointed physician in charge of the Boston Marine Hospital on this date. Dr. Waterhouse was the first to introduce the concept of interns and residents into hospitals in the United States.

February 27, 1813—A federal law encouraging vaccination against smallpox was approved on this date. The law was probably influenced by Thomas

Jefferson's earlier activities in this area, and it simply permitted the president to appoint an official agent to "preserve the genuine vaccine matter" and send it through the mail to anyone who requested it. However, in a good example of the problems often encountered by public health supporters of the time versus views that government should be involved in health issues only in times of emergency, the law was repealed in 1822.

October 12, 1842 — After decades of complaints about the quality of the water in New York City, the New York state legislature in 1834 authorized the city to plan an aqueduct and water system. On this date, a day celebrated by parades and the ringing of church bells, the city system bringing water from the Croton River was officially opened. The new system not only improved the quality of the drinking water but also the quantity. This permitted the installation of more flush toilets, and in three years connections to city sewers were permitted, followed by the construction of more sewers. It was a typical story in many cities of the time, but often there was a longer gap between the introduction of improved water supplies and the construction of improved sewage systems.

July 1846 — A young Hungarian doctor named Ignaz Phillipp Semmelweis, who had just celebrated his 28th birthday, was placed in charge of the First Obstetrical Clinic at the Vienna General Hospital. This clinic had a neonatal death rate due to puerperal fever of just over 13 percent, more than six times the 2 percent rate in the Second Obstetrical Clinic in the same hospital using the same techniques. The high rate in the first clinic was known to women who preferred to give birth in the street than to be brought to the hospital. The only difference in the two clinics was that the first was a teaching unit for medical students while the second had been selected in 1839 to instruct midwives.

Semmelweis was determined to find the reason for the difference in death rates between the two clinics, and the death of a friend in 1847 from an infection caused by a knife wound during a postmortem gave him the key clue. An autopsy of his friend showed a pathology similar to women dying from puerperal fever. The germ theory of disease was not known then, but Semmelweis concluded that some material was carried from cadavers to patients when students went from the autopsy room directly to the ward, as was the standard practice. He instituted a process of washing hands with chlorinated lime between autopsy work and visits to the clinic, and the death rate fell dramatically to nearly the same as that of the other clinic.

But Semmelweiss was a difficult man and given to lash out at his critics as murderers. He left Vienna, and in the early 1850s took charge of a maternity ward in his native Pest in Hungary. He instituted even more tightly controlled washing procedures there and reduced the death rate due to puerperal fever to an unheard of 0.85 percent. He made enemies at a great rate, and his work was never officially recognized by the time of his death in 1865. But before long his results began to speak for themselves, and with the development of the germ theory of disease and the recognition given him by Dr. Lister in England, Semmelweis became known as one of the pioneers of the germ theory and the first to practice antiseptic medicine.

November 1854—Florence Nightingale and her volunteer band of 38 nurses arrived in Scutari, Turkey, during this month. Nightingale was a well-born and well-educated English society belle who had chosen not to marry and had become interested in nursing near her 30th birthday in 1850. At the time there was no such thing as a paramedical nursing profession as we understand it today. In 1854, Nightingale offered to recruit and train and take to the Crimean war zone, where wounded British soldiers were "dying like flies" in the filthy Barracks Hospital at Scutari, 38 nurses who would help care for the soldiers. The British Secretary of War, who happened to be a social friend, accepted her offer, and Nightingale was on her way to becoming a legend in the field of nursing and public health.

Before her offer to go to Turkey, Nightingale in 1853 had become superintendent of the Institution for the Care of Sick Gentlewomen in Distressed Circumstances. There she practiced her beliefs that filth and dirt were the cause of all diseases, and that there was basically only one disease that was made steadily worse in conditions of poor sanitation. She held this belief until the end of her life in 1910 (at age 90), even when the germ theory of disease became well established by 1900. Nightingale is a good example of how a dedicated person can do a lot of good by working in an intelligent way even without fully understanding the basic theory behind the problem that is being attacked.

Nightingale and her nurses made a dramatic improvement in the conditions at Scutari. Their prime tools, other than greatly improved nutrition and sanitary care in the preparation and serving of food, were soap, water, brushes, mops, chlorine, lime, and other basic tools of sanitation applied constantly and consistently. Overcrowding was reduced, ventilation improved, and sanitary supplies increased. These supplies came from Nightingale's own considerable funds and those raised by readers of the *London Times*, who avidly followed the story of her progress. Nightingale supplemented other army services with other outside help as required. In six months at Scutari, Nightingale and her nurses reduced the death rate among the hospitalized soldiers from 42 to 22 per 1,000.

December 7, 1854—This was the date of the opening address to his students at Lille University by Louis Pasteur, after Pasteur had been appointed professor of chemistry and dean of the Faculty of Science. It was in this address that Pasteur made his oft-quoted statement that "chance favors only the mind which is prepared." Pasteur added that "without theory, practice is but routine born of habit. Theory alone can bring forth and develop the spirit of invention." These were concepts that Pasteur lived by, and they had much to do with his eventual substantial contributions to the germ theory of disease.

April 29, 1858— The second annual meeting of the Quarantine and Sanitary Convention was held on this day in Baltimore. This convention had delegates from various parts of the United States, but delegates from the Northeastern states were in the majority. The prime issue of the convention, which stretched into a third year in New York City in April 1859, was the then-common argument about whether quarantine made any sense in such diseases as cholera and yellow fever when there was no proof these diseases were contagious. The sense of the convention was that sanitation was the answer to all key health problems, and it voted 85–6 in its third year to recommend against quarantine for yellow fever. In four decades the recommendation would be proven correct, but debates such as this one would occupy much of the nineteenth century until the germ theory of disease was established by 1900.

June 1860— The first class of 15 trainees were enrolled in the Florence Nightingale School and Home for training nurses at St. Thomas' Hospital in London. Nightingale, in 1859, had written a book titled *Notes on Nursing: What It Is and What It Is Not*. The book became a common reference in English homes as well in class settings. Nightingale made a further impact on public health everywhere by designing hospitals using what became known as Florence Nightingale architecture. It featured various sanitary reforms with much emphasis on comparatively open and spacious areas to allow for good ventilation and to avoid overcrowding. Nightingale was an icon of the sanitation movement of the nineteenth century that also carried over into the early twentieth century.

January 1861— Dr. Oliver Wendell Holmes Sr., best known in the United States for his poetry, had published in this month a collection of his medical essays. Notable among these essays was one on "The Contagiousness of Puerperal Fever" originally published in 1843 and updated in 1855. Holmes was one of the first doctors in the United States to blame puerperal (childbirth) fever on doctors who went from patient to patient (or even from the dissecting room to patients) without bothering to wash their hands or change their filthy clothes. In this way they carried deadly microbes with them and delivered them to the next patient. Doctors generally were outraged to be told they were a major cause of such an ugly disease, and Holmes was attacked for his views. But Holmes was eventually proven to be correct. Later he was quoted as saying "an army of microbes marched up to support my position."

June 13, 1861— On this date, President Lincoln gave his approval to the creation of the United States Sanitary Commission. With the Civil War now underway, and the example of Florence Nightingale and the Crimean War not yet seven years in the past (*see entry for* November 1854), volunteers in the northern states started the commission in April 1861, and after initially rejecting the offer of the volunteers, Lincoln was persuaded to accept the group and give it legitimacy. The commission had a favorable impact not only on the northern side of the war but also on the entire nation in terms of public health. Their actions gave great impetus to the sanitation movement in the United States for the rest of the century.

It has been estimated that 600,000 men were killed in the Civil War, and that disease and illness due to the unsanitary conditions of the crowed camps on both sides, together with the lack of good nutrition and the lack of good food and water to consume, killed twice as many troops as did battle wounds. This means that two-thirds of all deaths were due to disease and illness. This kind of thing had been true in warfare for a long time and would not stop until World War II. There was a great deal of work for the Sanitary Commission to do, and the positive effects of their work would linger for many years, just as had been the case with Florence Nightingale in England.

April 20, 1862— Louis Pasteur and Claude Bernard completed the first test of what would come to be called pasteurization on this date. Pasteur had already shown that gentle heating before wine turned sour could kill various bacteria and molds present in the liquid. The process became most notably used to produce pure pasteurized milk around the world, but it applied to a number of different liquids and foods in general use and was first identified in conjunction with producing wine.

May 1, 1862— General Benjamin Butler of the Union army assumed formal military control of New Orleans on this date after the city had surrendered in late April. Butler's first general order was that all sanitary rules were to be strictly enforced, and a sanitary police force was organized to back up the order. As a southern port city, New Orleans had many outbreaks of yellow fever in its past, and a number of sanitary rules existed, but they had been poorly enforced. A labor force of two thousand men was employed to clean and drain the entire city. Stables, slaughterhouses, and "nuisance" industries were inspected regularly, and outhouses and garbage collection were closely supervised. The city would not be as clean again until the twentieth century. For almost seven years, there were no outbreaks of yellow fever, compared to a prior record of at least one minor outbreak every summer for the past 40 years. The rate of other diseases was also reduced. Butler had also imposed some strict quarantine rules, and in the postwar years there were fierce debates among the city fathers, as usual in those times, about whether sanitation or quarantine was the most meaningful step.

Regardless of the outcome of the sanitation versus quarantine debate, examples such as New Orleans gave great impetus to the sanitation movement in the United States, and together with the formation of the United States Sanitary Commission (*see entry for* July 13, 1861), the events of the Civil War, in spite of the deaths and destruction, proved to be a watershed in the development of public health in America. Many health boards were formed just after the Civil War (including perhaps the most famous of all in New York City), and public health became a much more professional field after the Civil War ended.

May 15, 1862— An act of Congress created the Department of Agriculture on this date. President Abraham Lincoln then appointed a chemist, Charles M. Wetherill, to the department to help in the process of screening agricultural commodities to be sure they were pure and unadulterated. This appointment grew into the Division of Chemistry and ultimately into the Food and Drug Administration (FDA).

August 12, 1865— Joseph Lister, a surgeon in London who had been greatly impressed by the early work of Louis Pasteur in identifying microbes as the cause of infection in surgery, began to put into practice certain techniques that would lead to antiseptic surgery. Lister published his techniques and results between March and July of 1867 (*see entry for* March 16, 1867).

February 20, 1866— On this date the Metropolitan Board of Health of New York City officially came into existence. A number of organizations had joined together to pressure the appropriate politicians to create the board, and it would prove to be very successful in pursuing public health issues from the day of its inception. The New York City board would be a model for many other health boards in the United States, and as the germ theory of disease developed in the late 1800s, it would lead in the United States, and even in the world, in terms of turning many of the new discoveries of the germ theory into practical action for the masses.

March 16, 1867— Joseph Lister published his initial article on this date in the medical journal *Lancet* describing his work on reducing the rate of infection in surgery by using carbolic acid and other procedures to be sure the surgery was conducted in an antiseptic manner. He used carbolic acid on surgical instruments, sprayed it on wounds and dressings, and incisions. He made all assistant doctors wear clean gloves and wash their hands repeatedly, all based on the desire to kill the microbes that Pasteur said were the cause of infection.

As might have been expected, his peers laughed at Lister. Many of his critics still believed in spontaneous generation, which Pasteur had disproved with an elegant experiment three years earlier in 1864. But Lister shrugged off his critics, and went on with his work, which was quite successful. Then Lister got real-world support from an unexpected source. In the brief Franco-Prussian War of 1870 both sides used what they called Listerism to reduce the rates of infection when surgery was performed on wounded soldiers. Lister became a hero on the continent, and French and German hospitals routinely practiced his techniques after the war. It was not until 1877, when Lister was appointed professor of surgery at King's College in London, that British doctors began to follow Lister's techniques. By then, the whole world, including the United States, was also doing so.

June 29, 1870— A bill on this date provided for the administration of marine hospitals within a bureau of the Treasury with a medical officer in charge. Less than a year later in April of 1871, Dr. John Maynard Woodward was appointed supervising surgeon of the Marine Hospital Service, marking the beginning of central control within the federal government of marine hospitals.

April 1872— Ten health reformers from New York and other cities held a meeting during this month to consider establishing a national organization called the American Public Health Association (APHA). At the time, there were about 100 city health boards, but only four states and the District of Columbia had health boards with a wider purview. Another meeting was held in September 1872 to gather more members, and a third meeting was scheduled for May 1873 to write a constitution and formalize the group. But it wasn't until November 1873 at a fourth meeting held in New York City that the final issues were resolved and the APHA came into existence. Some analysts feel that the creation of the APHA marked the true beginning of the professionalization of public health in the United States.

December 1, 1873— Regulations approved on this date covered the appointment and promotion of physicians in the Marine Hospital Service.

This established the first career service path for civilian employees in the federal government.

April 30, 1876— It was on this date that a previously unknown country doctor named Robert Koch began a three-day demonstration of the life cycle of the bacillus that produces anthrax. The demonstration was held in the laboratories of Ferdinand Cohn, a noted expert in Germany and all of Europe on bacteriology. Several well-known scientists were present at the demonstration, and all agreed Koch's work was a great step forward in bacteriology and the development of the germ theory of disease. Six years later Koch would gain worldwide fame for discovering the bacteria that causes tuberculosis.

April 29, 1878— The first Federal Quarantine Legislation was passed on this date. Eight months later, on December 21, Congress appropriated funds for investigating the origin and causes of epidemic diseases, especially yellow fever and cholera. There was already doubt in some places that yellow fever, at least, was not a contagious disease that could be passed from person to person and thus quarantine was inappropriate.

April 30, 1878— In an address to the French Academy of Medicine on his ongoing work on the germ theory of disease and related matters, Louis Pasteur reiterated his position that surgeons should be extra conscious of cleanliness in their work, making sure everything that came in contact with their surgery was clean, including instruments, various surfaces, their hands, and bandages and cloths used to cover wounds. Pointing out the ubiquity of microbes, he recommended heating air and water at high temperatures to kill the microbes. It was a message similar to that of the sanitarians except that Pasteur had a specific medical theory and hypothesis behind his recommendations. It was this part of Pasteur's work that had led Joseph Lister in England a decade ago to develop the technique of antiseptic surgery that would finally spread around the world after Lister was appointed professor of surgery at King's College in London in 1877.

July 9, 1878— Louis Pasteur presented a report to the French Academy of Medicine on the bacterial transmission of anthrax, his most recent discovery. Even at this late date, Pasteur felt compelled to add an attack on those who still held that bacteria and such arose from spontaneous generation. Before the members of the Academy of Science in 1864, Pasteur had shown in an elegant demonstration using cleverly arranged glass tubes and flasks that nothing grew in the broth in the flasks which were exposed to air, but not to the bacteria in the air which could not get past the filtering arranged in the tubes. It should have been the final proof of the germ theory of disease, but nearly 15 years later everyone had not yet seen the light. Pasteur was constantly on the attack against what we would call today junk science.

March 3, 1879—A law was passed creating the National Board of Health on this day. The creation of this board represented the first organized, national medical research effort of the federal government in the United States. The new board of health was a response to the 1878 epidemic of yellow fever that had ravaged every southern port city and a good part of the Mississippi Valley.

November 22, 1879—A group of health and sanitary experts from the recently created National Board of Health (*see entry for* March 3, 1879) met in Memphis on this date at the request of the city of Memphis. The city had suffered severely in the epidemic of yellow fever that began in 1878, had a reputation as one of the filthiest cities in the nation, and in 1872 had the highest death rate of any major city in the country (46.6 per 1,000). The city was losing population due to these problems.

The invited experts immediately told the city it needed a new sewer program, and while actions were being taken in the state legislature to begin such a program, a health inspection and survey of Memphis was made. The survey results were devastating. Over 20 percent of the buildings and homes in the city had cellars that were poorly ventilated or damp or else had standing water in them. Only 215 of the buildings in the city were connected to the privately owned sewer system. The sanitation force of the city was inadequate for the task, and the privately owned water works was bankrupt. Most citizens used cisterns or shallow wells dug too close to outhouses as a basic water supply.

A plan was made to redo nearly everything, and ten years later in 1889, the death rate in Memphis had fallen from the 46.6 level noted in 1872 to 21.5 in 1889. Memphis became an example of how health conditions could be improved in a city by relatively simple, although perhaps expensive, steps.

June 1880—William Crawford Gorgas, a newly minted doctor, entered the United States Army Medical Corps as a lieutenant. Gorgas had dreamed of entering the army via West Point, but his father, an army officer, had defected to join his fellow southern officers in the south when the Civil War broke out. Both Gorgas and his future wife had yellow fever and thus both were immune to the disease after they recovered. Accordingly, Gorgas was often stationed in places where yellow fever was a problem. Gorgas ended up stationed at Siboney, the army's yellow-fever camp outside Havana, during the Spanish-American War in 1898.

Gorgas believed, as did Florence Nightingale, that filth rather than microbes carried by mosquitoes was the real cause of yellow fever. When Gorgas was appointed sanitary officer of Havana in 1898, he used fire and manpower to clear the swamps and to make Havana one of the cleanest cities in the Western Hemisphere. Not only did he wipe out yellow fever but many other infectious diseases as well. The overall death rate in Havana fell by 60 percent. Gorgas would later take his disease-fighting talents to the canal zone in 1906.

May 1882— During this month, Robert Koch, a German doctor who did a great deal of chemical research and did much to help produce the germ theory of diseases, discussed before the Berlin Physiological Society his isolation of the bacteria that causes tuberculosis. Koch's work caused a sensation around the world, because tuberculosis was one of mankind's greatest killers and it was hoped the isolation of the germ that caused it would lead to a vaccine. The hope for the rapid development of a truly effective vaccine was not realized, but the knowledge that it was a communicable disease helped to develop actions that greatly reduced the number of deaths caused by tuberculosis before the development of the antibiotic streptomycin in the 1940s.

Koch's work also supported the efforts that led to a chain of announcements over the next two decades that identified the cause of nearly all the prime bacterial diseases known to man.

July 12, 1884— To demonstrate how difficult it was to get the medical establishment to accept the idea of the germ theory of disease, the edition of the *Journal of the American Medical Association* published on this date carried an editorial disparaging Robert Koch's recent isolation of the bacteria that causes cholera (this was after Koch had isolated the microbe that causes tuberculosis). The writer called the germ theory "greatly exaggerated" by the press and complained that, in essence, the germ theory was causing "fear, dread, and mental trepidation" among the public.

September 22, 1884— In a letter on this date in reply to a letter received from Dom Pedro II, the emperor of Brazil, Louis Pasteur confirmed that he had developed a type of vaccine for rabies (more a cure than a preventative vaccine), but he was reluctant to test it on humans. Maybe the head of a government could arrange a test on convict volunteers who could be offered life in prison rather than execution if they volunteered. Pasteur was not able to arrange such a test, but just over nine months later a test was forced on Pasteur that made him famous worldwide.

January 29, 1885— Louis Pasteur told the Academie Françoise, in connection with his studies on a vaccine for rabies, that he suspected the existence of what we now know to be the antibody/antigen relationship. Pasteur said there might be a general relationship, and if so, it would be a "stupendous discovery." Once more he was right in his hypothesis and was once again far ahead of his time.

April 3, 1885—The highly regarded New York City Board of Health passed a resolution on this date saying that the "laying of all telegraph wires underground in one season would prove highly detrimental to the health of the city" because of the "noxious gases" that would be released from the soil. This was a good example of how the sanitarians still believed that "miasmas," mysterious noxious gases from unearthed soil, swamps, and sewers were themselves responsible for causing disease. As late as 1900 various health boards would prevent gas and water companies from digging up the streets in warm weather for fear that a potentially dangerous miasma would be released. It was not until the twentieth century that most sanitarians would accept the germ theory of disease. Some, like the famous Florence Nightingale, would never accept it in their lifetimes.

July 4, 1885—On this day a nine-year-old schoolboy named Joseph Meister was bitten by a rabid dog while Meister was on his way to school in Meissengott, France. The local doctor told his mother to take the boy to Paris where there was a man named Pasteur who might offer some help. Otherwise the boy was doomed to die a horrible death.

Two days later the boy was brought to Pasteur, and because Pasteur was not officially a doctor but only a chemist, Pasteur called in two doctors to assist him and officially prescribe treatment. The doctors both prescribed Pasteur's rabies treatment, which had been tested only on animals so far, as the only hope. Pasteur began the treatment and was rewarded with success when the boy was sent home well on July 23, only 17 days later.

July 23, 1885—Ironically, when Joseph Meister went home on this date cured by Pasteur of rabies, the date also effectively marked the end of Pasteur's great scientific career as a researcher. The news of the first-ever rabies cure electrified the world. Patients and reporters poured into Paris from everywhere. Public subscriptions and government funds set up the new Pasteur Institute by 1888 (including some foreign branches), an institute headed by Pasteur that provided laboratories for medical and biological research and manufactured vaccines. The Pasteur Institute continued to do advanced work in its field. But Pasteur was already somewhat frail, and he was much in demand, which made it hard to do concentrated research work. Pasteur's birthday became a national holiday. Pasteur lived until 1895 and died a celebrity.

August 1887— During this month a bacteriological laboratory known as the Laboratory of Hygiene was established at the marine hospital on Staten Island in New York. Dr. Joseph J. Kinyoun was in charge, and the laboratory was specifically intended to do research on cholera and other infectious diseases. The laboratory was renamed simply the Hygienic Laboratory in 1891 and was then moved to Washington, D.C. It would eventually play a key part in public health service of the future as it became the National Institute(s) of Health (NIH).

December 25, 1891— On this Christmas night, a child in Berlin was the first known person in the world to be treated for diphtheria using what was called diphtheria antitoxin. It had been discovered by intensive research (primarily by some Frenchmen who had been co-workers with Louis Pasteur) that the diphtheria bacteria per se did not cause the damage produced by the disease, but rather the bacteria gave off a poison or toxin that attacked the body. It was possible to gather an antitoxin from the blood or serum of affected animals (usually horses) that destroyed the toxin produced by the diphtheria bacteria and thus essentially produced a cure. The Christmas child in Berlin was the first to be so cured.

September 9, 1892— The New York City Board of Health, at the urging of Dr. Hermann Biggs, established the Division of Pathology, Bacteriology, and Disinfection and placed it under the direction of Dr. Biggs. This division was one of the first examples of how the New York City Board of Health applied the discoveries of the germ theory of disease to the public at large. Dr. Biggs immediately began to use the division to confirm suspected immigrant cases of cholera using a method he had devised to isolate the causative bacteria.

In addition, Dr. Biggs convinced the board to appoint Dr. William H. Park to make a positive analysis of diphtheria cases to weed out the false cases and eliminate unnecessary disinfections and quarantines. The laboratory expanded into producing high-grade smallpox vaccine and diphtheria antitoxin.

September 30, 1893— The Michigan State Board of Health voted on this date to require the reporting of tuberculosis cases to local health officers. Similar efforts were made in Baltimore and Philadelphia around this time. It was felt that such reports would help control the spread of the disease. However, for many years to come, this would not be an easy rule to enforce. At the time few people wanted it known that they or a family member had tuberculosis, as it was often considered a terminal disease. On a more practical basis, many life insurance companies had a clause in their contracts to the effect that no funds would be paid if the cause of death was identified as tuberculosis. Doctors were understandably reluctant to betray their patients by identifying them as having tuberculosis, especially in cases where the doctor's payment for his final services would come from a life insurance policy.

September 4, 1894 — Emile Roux, a Frenchman who had been a co-worker with Pasteur, gave a paper at the Eighth International Congress of Hygiene and Demography in Budapest that elaborated on the concept of diphtheria antitoxin, which Roux had been studying for several years. This paper triggered a general interest in the subject, especially in the United States. The antitoxin approach at least permitted a cure for the dreaded disease, and it was the starting point from which a protective vaccination would eventually be developed in the early twentieth century by doctor William H. Park and others in the New York City Department of Health.

June 30, 1895 — The agricultural appropriation bill for the fiscal year ending on this date contained $10,000 to enable the secretary of agriculture "to investigate and report upon the nutritive value of the various articles and commodities used for human food," with special suggestions to be made for "full, wholesome, and edible rations that were less wasteful and more economical than those in common use." The amount of money in the next year was increased to $15,000. It was a noble attempt to add nutrition to the list of items being investigated in the name of public heath. The U.S. Department of Agriculture made an intensive attempt to comply, surveying the diets of various groups in the population. But this was before vitamins had been discovered (*see entry for* December 1911), and the recommendations fell far short of what we know today about good nutrition. Still, the attempt was praiseworthy, and future recommendations would prove to be far more useful.

October 1895 — The laboratory division of the New York City Department of Health (*see entry for* September 9, 1892) had become so successful and so large it was forced to move to find more space. It had drawn national and international attention for its skilled production of diphtheria antitoxin, and ten other cities had copied the New York model and established laboratories as part of their health departments. Soon it was impossible to think of health departments without laboratories to diagnose diseases, although some local physicians began to complain about what they saw as unfair competition from local governments.

August 27, 1897 — Ronald Ross, a British Army surgeon serving in India, on this date confirmed that a mosquito carrier was responsible for spreading malaria. This discovery would eventually lead to a great public health/environmental battle in the middle of the twentieth century over the use of DDT to eliminate malaria-carrying mosquitoes around the world, and the damage the long-lasting DDT would do to the environment.

December 8, 1900— A soldier who had volunteered to be bitten by a mosquito from a yellow fever ward came down with yellow fever on this date. Dr. Walter Reed, in charge of The United States Army Yellow Fever Commission was jubilant. After a series of careful experiments, it was the final proof to Reed that yellow fever was carried and spread by specific types of mosquitoes. Reed died of peritonitis following an appendectomy in 1902 and never found the virus that caused yellow fever. In Reed's time, diseases like yellow fever were thought to be caused by ultramicroscopic bacterium. It would be some time before viruses such as the one that causes yellow fever could actually be seen. But the key finding was how yellow fever was spread not what the causative agent looked like.

February 1901— A Yellow Fever Commission agreed during this month to follow the recommendations of Walter Reed and his co-workers (*see entry for* December 8, 1900) to eliminate yellow fever. Those recommendations primarily included eliminating the mosquitoes that carried the disease by eliminating their breeding grounds and protecting the already sick from being bitten by mosquitoes that could further transmit the disease. Measures along these lines were implemented in Havana, and by September 1901, yellow fever had been wiped out there, never to return.

July 1, 1902— The Marine Hospital Service was officially renamed the Public Health and Marine Hospital Service. Essentially for the first time, the law was specifically intended to designate a bureau of the federal government as an agency in which public health matters could be coordinated. An accompanying law, known as the Biological Control Act, authorized the Public Health and Marine Hospital Service to regulate the sale or transport for human use of viruses, serums, vaccines, antitoxins, and related products in interstate traffic or as imported from any foreign country into the United States.

June 1904— Following a preliminary meeting in Baltimore in January, the National Association for the Study and Prevention of Tuberculosis was formed in Atlantic City, New Jersey, during this month (in 1918, the name would be shortened to the National Tuberculosis Association). The first president of the association was Edward L. Trudeau, the physician who had pioneered the sanatorium treatment for tuberculosis. By 1907, in order to help with financing, it had been decided to sell special stamps or seals. Initially sold in conjunction with the Red Cross, from 1919 on the association would sell Christmas seals on its own and by 1947 would raise $19 million in this way. Many other groups would follow the National Tuberculosis Association model in trying to raise money for a specific disease, but the practice began in Atlantic City in 1904.

August 1905— By the end of this month, a major yellow fever outbreak in New Orleans was stopped by an anti-mosquito program coordinated by the Public Health and Marine Hospital Service in conjunction with the health boards of Louisiana and New Orleans. The anti-mosquito program used the techniques learned initially in the Spanish-American War of 1898. The New Orleans success marked the first time in the United States that a yellow fever epidemic had been stopped before the onset of cooler weather.

June 30, 1906— The Food and Drug Act was passed, authorizing the federal government to monitor the purity of foods and the safety of medicines. The Department of Agriculture and its Bureau of Chemistry assumed this responsibility. The name of the bureau was changed to the Food, Drug, and Insecticide Administration in July 1917, and it was then shortened to the Food and Drug Administration (FDA) in July 1930.

June 20, 1909— The *New York American,* a sensationalistic newspaper owned by William Randolph Hearst, carried a story on this date about "Typhoid Mary." The woman was actually named Mary Mellon, an unmarried Irish immigrant who came to the United States in the 1880s as a young teenager. She was working as a cook for rich families in 1906 at the age of 37 when she was carefully tracked and identified as the source of an outbreak of typhoid among her employers in the New York City area. Mellon turned out to be one of those rare persons who could be a carrier for a disease but not suffer ill effects personally. After she was found to carry the bacteria that caused typhoid, she was kept in isolation in a hospital. But all the drugs available then could not cure her of the disease, and she refused to have her gall bladder removed, a procedure that sometimes stopped the production of the typhus bacilli. She refused to believe she carried the disease, and she refused to learn the relatively simple hygienic procedures necessary to could keep her from spreading the disease (typhoid was spread in food and water by contact with stools and urine from carriers). Mellon was eventually kept in isolation at a hospital on an island where she essentially lived alone in a bungalow on the grounds.

When her story became known, offers of aid poured in, and she got the services of a lawyer. A judge refused to release her, as it was legal to hold infected persons in quarantine. However, a softhearted health commissioner decided he had made her understand the danger she represented, and he believed her promises not to cook or handle foods for others and to otherwise observe proper hygienic procedures. Mary Mallon was released on her own recognizance on February 19, 1910, promising to check in with the Bureau of Health every three months. She had been held in isolation just over three years.

In spite of her promises, Mary Mallon immediately disappeared and went underground, changing her name several times and taking up her old occupation as a cook. She was eventually recaptured following some outbreaks of typhoid in 1915 that were ultimately tracked back to "Typhoid Mary." At the age of 48 she was held in detention at her previous island hospital, and this time she stayed in detention for the rest of her life. She died at the age of 69 in 1938. She claimed her plight was due to a British conspiracy because she wanted to free her homeland from British rule, but no evidence of such a conspiracy ever came to light. Today her problem could be readily cured with antibiotics. But at a time when such drugs did not exist, the strange nature of her body that permitted her to carry typhoid without suffering its effects and her refusal to take the precautions necessary to avoid spreading the disease doomed her to an isolated existence. At a minimum, she caused 53 cases of typhoid with three deaths. The probable count was much higher. A tragic case of the times.

October 26, 1909— The Rockefeller Foundation in New York City created the Sanitary Commission to Exterminate Hookworm Disease and provided it with one million dollars to be spent over the next five years. The main focus of the program was the South. This effort was a good example of how public health services were now beginning to focus also on health problems in mostly rural areas in the United States.

May 22, 1910— This date marked the brightest portion of the great show put on by Halley's Comet over the United States. Many people do not know that the man for whom Halley's Comet is named, Edmund Halley, published one of the first tables of life expectancy in 1693. Halley was an actuarian involved in life insurance. He examined the headstones in graveyards and used other records to determine that life expectancy at birth in Europe at the time was 33 years. Life expectancy at age 80 was six years. Over 300 years later, life expectancy at birth is approaching 80, but life expectancy at 80 is still less than 10 years. Life expectancy overall has greatly increased because of the elimination of early deaths due to infectious diseases, but the expected extra years for the elderly has increased very little because the maximum life span has increased very little, if at all. Edmund Halley was only an amateur astronomical observer, but he is known today for his discovery of Halley's Comet, not for his work calculating life expectancies.

The show put on by Halley's Comet in 1910 was truly spectacular. It covered a good portion of the sky and was easily visible to everyone in the United States (its return in 1985 was a complete dud, thus making it hard for people of this age to understand the excitement the comet caused in 1910). The time of Halley's Comet in 1910 was an opportunity for a number of hoaxes of the type that have always plagued public heath officials. The problem began when the Yerkes observatory in Chicago used spectroscopy to determine that the tail of the comet contained some poisonous cyanogen gas. Some people panicked when they realized that it was predicted the earth would pass through the comet's tail, and these people assumed they would be exposed to poisonous gas. People were reported to have committed suicide because of this fear, and an urban legend grew up around a group in Oklahoma that attempted to sacrifice a virgin to avert the "catastrophe."

Various entrepreneurs offered comet pills and comet insurance to the gullible. Some charlatans worked both sides of the street by offering for sale special glasses that would enable the user to see through women's clothing at the time of passing through the tail of the comet, and then selling women's underwear that would block such a view. When the earth was reported to be passing through the tail of the comet on May 19, fears reached their height and many churches held all-night prayer services. At the other end of the spectrum, hotels held comet watching events, and a man named C.B. Harmon offered college deans an opportunity to join him in viewing the spectacle from a balloon.

After the view peaked on Sunday, May 22, the comet faded from the headlines of the newspapers, and the entrepreneurs who had offered pills and insurance could claim that their products worked as intended. The event of Halley's Comet in 1910 was not the first nor the last time hoaxes were perpetrated to separate gullible people from their money for fears relating to their health, but it was certainly one of the most spectacular events in the United States to be surrounded by the usual hoax entrepreneurs and their victims.

September 1910— The Joint Board of Sanitary Control in the Cloak, Suit, and Skirt Industry of Greater New York began the study and control of health conditions in clothing factories and shops. It was the first time in American industrial history that an employer's association and a union tried to establish and enforce healthful working conditions. Similar operations sprung up after the Triangle Waist Factory fire the next year in 1911 claimed 145 lives, mostly young women.

December 1911— Casimir Funk, a Jewish chemist in Poland, announced the isolation of a definite chemical substance aiding nutrition that he named a "vitamine." His name stuck, although the final "e" was dropped when further such substances were found not to belong to the amine family as Funk first thought. But the concept was established that certain vitamins were necessary for health, and that a deficiency disease lacking a vitamin could be established and then cured by adding the vitamin.

Over the next two decades, a number of vitamins were discovered, and the precedent of labeling them by letters of the alphabet was established. The causes of diseases like rickets (lack of adequate vitamin D) and pellagra (lack of adequate vitamin B) were discovered, and in 1917 the public health departments of Massachusetts and New York became the first to have nutritionists as part of their public health services.

August 14, 1912— The name of the Public Health and Marine Hospital Service was changed to simply the Public Health Service (PHS), coming full cycle from the original bill establishing a relief service for seamen in 1798. The legislation greatly broadened the charter of the PHS to include "diseases of man" and contributing factors such as pollution of navigable streams and the dissemination of applicable information.

October 5, 1912— An article in the *New York Times* of this date reported on the annual meeting of the American Association for the Study and Prevention of Infant Mortality. One physician at the meeting decried the fact that the United States ranked in the lower half of 31 "civilized countries" in terms of infant mortality rates. The doctor further stated that infant mortality rates were the "most sensitive" test of civilization. He claimed that if babies were properly born and cared for, their "death rate would be negligible."

The doctor exaggerated to some degree because a large percentage of infant mortality cases was due to birth defects and premature births, neither of which medicine of the time could favorably impact in any significant way. However, what really was at issue in this era was the "milk question." Many studies have shown that the biggest factor in the death rate of infants and toddlers in this period was gastrointestinal illness (basically diarrhea). Breast-fed babies had a much lower death rate than those fed otherwise. In addition to the question of whether the milk itself was contaminated, many mothers were not properly taught how to sterilize bottles and nipples and how to care for their infants when they did have diarrhea.

Many cities, led by New York City and it excellent department of health, set up milk stations where mothers could come and get pasteurized milk in bottles and also get instruction about how to keep the milk and bottles and nipples clean and how to care for the child in general. Alternatives like milk dips, where milk was brought in from the country in uncooled cans and the milk ladled out with a common dipper, were much more likely to contain undesirable bacteria. Even bottled milk from dairies had many opportunities to get bacterially contaminated between the cow and the baby, let alone to be contaminated at the source.

These relatively simple milk stations and their influence on mothers greatly reduced infant mortality between the late nineteenth century and the early twentieth century. Great medical advances, except perhaps for diphtheria antitoxin, were not the prime mover in this area. For example, the mortality rate for diarrheal diseases for children ages 1 to 4 in Philadelphia in 1870 was 41.4 per 1,000. By 1900, 30 years later, it had fallen to 21.6; in yet another 30 years in 1930, it was down to 5.4. The rates for infants were higher, but the reduction at each interval was even greater.

February 6, 1913—An article appeared in the *Boston Medical and Surgical Journal* of this date concerning the functions of the so-called free dispensary. There had been an ongoing controversy about dispensaries in the United States since before the beginning of the twentieth century. Dispensaries were sort of an early emergency room service for the poor, but mainly only prescriptions were dispensed (filled by an on-site pharmacy) after a brief examination. There were complaints from the medical establishment that patients who could afford to pay for medical care were abusing the system by seeking treatment at the free dispensaries. There were arguments from the other side that the doctors who donated time to the dispensaries and used them to teach medical students treated the patients roughly, making them wait for a long time and giving them very brief examinations except for "interesting" cases. Dispensaries finally faded away as hospitals rose to eminence in the rest of the twentieth century.

July 13, 1913—The magazine *Women's Home Companion* of this date carried an item about "Better Babies." The magazine stated that Better Babies "is on the tongue of half the mothers in America." With the *Women's Home Companion* playing a key promotional role, Better Babies contests enjoyed a brief popularity in the United States in 1913 and 1914. The contests began at state fairs in the Midwest, then spread to cities and towns across the country. Showing their state fair origin, the contests were sometimes known as human stock shows. There were judging rules and examinations, and points were awarded to contestants not unlike those used in judging cattle. Some public health benefits were claimed as some focused on the need to reduce infant mortality. But like most fads, the movement faded quickly, especially when the magazine decided some other fad could sell more copies.

April 14, 1914— A group of physicians who were directors of industrial medical departments formed the Conference Board of Physicians in Industry. This organization became the prime advisor on medical problems in industry to the National Industrial Conference Board. This activity was part of a movement that saw the practice of medical examinations for employees begin at Sears, Roebuck Company of Chicago in 1909 and the beginning of effective workman's compensation in 1910.

June 13, 1914— William Crawford Gorgas, the hero of yellow fever in the 1898 Spanish-American War (*see entry for* June 1880), who had been appointed surgeon general of the army by President Wilson in February 1914, published an article in the *Journal of the American Medical Association* on this date, describing the subsequent work he did in the canal zone starting in 1906, following his efforts in the Spanish-American War of 1898.

He said his main problem in the canal zone was actually pneumonia among the mostly black workers brought in from the West Indies to complete the Panama Canal. In one year, using the techniques of improved housing and corresponding greatly reduced crowding, and higher wages permitting much improved nutrition, the death rate fell by 43 percent. By August 1913, the pneumonia death rate among the black workers had fallen by 97.8 percent, and the absolute pneumonia death rate among everyone, black and white, in the canal zone was below four per 100,000 compared to 131 per 100,000 on the mainland.

Gorgas had completed an experiment in public health showing clearly that such simple things as greatly improved living conditions could substantially reduce death rates from infectious diseases. But he continued to support research for a vaccine against pneumonia, because he stated, as had so many others before him, that a preventative vaccine was far superior to trying to stop the spread of the disease after the fact.

Summer 1916— There was a polio epidemic in the United States that drew strong attention to the disease for the first time in the twentieth century. It was an epidemic only in the sense that there many more polio cases than before, but in total it was still a small amount compared to other infectious diseases. But even if small by comparison, 27,000 people were paralyzed in 1916 and 6,000 died. There were random epidemics with many fewer victims in later years, but the disease did not peak until 1952 when 58,000 cases were reported. After the Salk vaccine was introduced, the reported cases fell to 3,000 by the end of the 1950s, and soon the disease was essentially gone.

Even though polio was not very prevalent compared to other infectious diseases at any time in the first half of the twentieth century, and it didn't seem to appear nearly at all in the United States until the twentieth century began, polio is an ancient disease. The prime problem with polio was that it struck small children, even toddlers, and left them paralyzed for life. For this reason, it was greatly feared by parents.

The irony about polio is that it is believed in retrospect to have been caused in the United States by the same sanitation movement that was trying to prevent infectious diseases. The theory is that in less sanitized conditions where open sewers and overflowing cesspools were common, nearly all children got polio in infancy when the disease rarely produces paralytic effects. No one may even notice the disease among all the fevers and small illnesses of infancy. But having had polio in infancy means an individual was afterwards immune for life. When the sanitation movement removed the exposure to sewage and the like, children did not first contact polio until they were older and more susceptible to paralysis. The disease is believed to be spread by direct contact with persons who wash their hands improperly and infrequently after fecal contact. This is why children were a prime target of the polio virus.

But polio would be conquered in the early 1950s due to an unusual combination of a popular president with the disease who caused enough private funds to be raised to not only care for patients like himself but to provide additional funding for research that eventually created a vaccine.

May 1917—Now that the United States was officially involved in World War I, President Woodrow Wilson authorized the Army Medical Department to organize a sanitary corps to work with the troops. The Public Health Service was heavily involved, and their key action was an antimosquito program to eliminate malaria around the many camps and defense industries located in the South. Drawing on recent experience in Panama, the program was intended to eliminate mosquitoes in a belt one mile wide around the areas being protected. Malaria was not a problem in the camps, and as a corollary benefit, the incidence of malaria fell sharply in civilian areas as well.

January 1918—Nine months after the United States had entered World War I, the surgeon general of the army, Dr. William Crawford Gorgas, who was famous for vanquishing yellow fever, malaria, and pneumonia in Havana and the canal zone earlier in the century (*see entry for* June 13, 1914), testified before the Senate Military Affairs Committee. Gorgas had made a personal tour of the military camps around the country based on reports coming into his office on the incidence of infectious diseases in the camps. Gorgas advised that the general mobilization now taking place be delayed "two or three months" until adequate preparations could be made. Camp hospitals and related facilities needed to be built and adequate personnel found to run them.

Otherwise, Gorgas stated, the overcrowded conditions in the camps would make "disastrous contagious diseases inevitable."

Gorgas, who credited his past successes primarily to implementing sanitary procedures and controlling overcrowding, was stating the obvious in his mind, but his testimony was politically incorrect at the time. Great efforts were being made to mobilize American troops and get them overseas where World War I was felt to be entering a critical stage. Gorgas conveniently reached his mandatory retirement age in October, and he was forced to retire just when the ravages of the flu/pneumonia epidemic of 1918 were beginning to reach a peak, both in the military camps and in the general public.

March 21, 1918— The Germans launched an offensive on this date that in three weeks overran 1,250 square miles of France. On March 23, they began shelling Paris, only 75 miles away, with their Big Bertha howitzer. A disaster seemed imminent to the western allies. About 84,000 American troops left for Europe in March, and another 118,00 in April, to attempt to repulse the Germans. With this news crowding the headlines, initial signs that some sort of epidemic was beginning in the United States were easily overlooked.

In March, over 1,000 workers at the Ford Motor Company in Detroit had to be sent home with the flu. In April and May, 500 of the 1900 prisoners at San Quentin Prison in California came down with the flu. There were other isolated outbreaks, but public health services, both on the federal and state levels, were not nearly as well-organized as they would be after the war, and not enough good records were being kept. Only in places like prisons and military camps where attendance was not voluntary and where those falling ill had to be cared for were good records kept. Thus, no general alarm bell was ringing, at least not one big enough to push the war news aside.

April 1918— A review of the death records of a flu epidemic that rode through Louisville, Kentucky, in this month showed a new phenomenon that would become typical of the flu pandemic of 1918 as it traveled around the world. Normally, when flu struck, a plot of the number of deaths versus age would be U-shaped, with the most deaths occurring among the very young and the very old. The plot in this case was shaped like a W, with a big spike added for those around 30 years old, supposedly in the prime of life. Thus, the pneumonia associated with the flu was not only especially deadly, it was killing people who should have been most resistant. Many theories have been advanced to explain this, but none are fully satisfactory, and the phenomenon was not seen before or since the flu epidemic of 1918.

July 9, 1918— The Chamberlain-Kahn Act added venereal disease (which often increases dramatically in times of war such as World War I in which the United States was now deeply involved) to the list of public health issues to be studied by the Public Health Service.

August 16, 1918— The surgeon general of the United States issued an order to the Public Health Service (PHS) on this date saying that those medical officers in charge of quarantine operation should be especially vigilant in holding ships from Europe on which flu cases existed in quarantine until the local public health authorities had been notified. The navy on August 9 had issued a precautionary bulletin warning that flu was now at high levels in Europe, Hawaii, and elsewhere. The bulletin included symptoms, the incubation period, and treatment. The order to the PHS was necessary because the PHS generally had little authority at the time. It could not order quarantine on its own for such a normally mild disease like the flu, and even if it could, the tremendous volume of port activities going on for the war effort would have made it politically impossible to enforce. Actually, the worldwide deluge of flu about to come probably could not have been stopped by any administrative action.

September 23, 1918— Colonel William Henry Welch, a distinguished pathologist, scientist, and physician who was an ex-president of both the American Medical Association and the Association of American Physicians and several other such prestigious groups, arrived on this date at Camp Devens, about 30 miles west of Boston. Welch, who had left his position at John Hopkins to enlist in the military with men half and even a third his age to help fight the war, was a troubleshooter for the surgeon general of the Army. He concentrated on the fight against infectious diseases in military camps. He was ready to retire to civilian service when he was asked to check out horrendous reports coming in from the Boston area about an epidemic of what was being called the Spanish flu.

Camp Devens had about 45,000 men in a camp originally intended for 35,000, and it was preparing to send most of them to France to follow the 35,000 it had sent previously in the first year of its existence. But beginning in early September, soldiers began to show up on sick call. By September 18 there were 6,674 cases of influenza, with 1,176 showing up on that day alone. More ominously, this flu seemed to have an unusually high percentage of associated complications of pneumonia. Flu is a major inconvenience, but pneumonia kills (no flu epidemic before or since that of 1918 has had such a propensity for pneumonic complications).

When Dr. Welch arrived, Camp Devens had had 12,064 cases of flu reported since early in the month. Almost 2,000 cases of pneumonia were involved, and just on the day Welch had arrived, 66 men died of pneumonia. The Camp Devens hospital was built to accommodate 2,000 men, but now

8,000 needed cover and treatment. In the morgue, bodies were stacked like cordwood, and when Dr. Welch performed autopsies, he was stunned at the conditions of the lungs of the dead men. Even in his vast experience, he had never seen such circumstances.

Dr. Welch and his associates could only recommend that no more troops be sent to Devens, and the men there should be sent nowhere else. As soon as possible, the camp capacity should be reduced by 10,000 to relieve future overcrowding. With the war going on, there was no way to implement these suggestions. The flu epidemic played out in this fashion in the military for the next few months until the war ended on November 11, 1918. By the end of October, over 17,000 men at Camp Devens, over a third of the entire camp, came down with flu. Of this total, 787 died of pneumonia. Eventually, the flu epidemic would kill nearly as many military men as combat (about 50,000), at least ten times more that number of civilians (over half a million), and more than twice as many people around the world (over 20 million) as died on all fronts in the entire four years of the war).

September 26, 1918— Even with American forces pushing ever deeper into the Argonne in Europe and General Pershing calling for reinforcements, the planned October draft call of 142,000 men was cancelled on this date because nearly all of the camps to which the men were to report were quarantined due to the flu. A follow-up call of 78,000 additional men planned during October was also postponed, but no one realized the war would end in seven weeks and the men would not be needed anyway. But the fight against the flu in the United States was a constantly raging battle.

September 27, 1918— On this date, the Red Cross headquarters in Washington, D.C., wired all its division directors of nursing to mobilize against the flu. Even though the Volunteer Medical Service Corps (VMSC), a sort of backup organization to the Public Health Service (PHS), was in the process of putting over 600 doctors in the field (from a list of 72,000 volunteers who were otherwise ineligible for military service and who paid a fee of one dollar to apply), the big need was for nurses. There were no medical weapons against the flu except good care. Right away 1500 nurses volunteered to fight the flu before money was appropriated to pay them. But even this was not enough, and the Red Cross urged women with no prior professional service to volunteer. On October 5, the PHS chief in Boston was forced to wire his counterpart in Bath, Maine, saying, "I can send you all the doctors you want, but not a single nurse." Still, without so many volunteers, the situation would have been far worse.

Also, around this time of civilian mobilization, a new song appeared in the press that schoolgirls were supposedly singing as they skipped rope at school in Massachusetts (it later was attributed to nearly everywhere in the country):

> I had a little bird
> And its name was Enza.
> I opened the window
> And in-flew-Enza.

September 28, 1918—On this date, about 200,000 people gathered to view the parade stretching over 23 city blocks that kicked off the Fourth Liberty Loan Drive in Philadelphia. This conflux of people was in spite of news about a gathering flu epidemic in the city. It was typical of many cities in the country around this time. Patriotic fervor was high, and great crowds came out to support the bond drives needed to conduct the war, in spite of the high probability of catching the flu from the packed crowds. Ironically, the war would be over in six weeks, but there was no way to know that at the time.

October 3, 1918—Only five days after the parade on September 28, the flu was exploding through Philadelphia. On this date, the city ordered the closing of all schools, churches, theaters, and other places of public amusement. The same day, the acting state commissioner of health extended the order of closure of places of public amusement (including saloons) in all cities in Pennsylvania, leaving the closing of schools and churches up to local option. The next day, the surgeon general of the Public Health System recommended that all state health officers across the country follow the lead of Pennsylvania.

October 7, 1918—With 850 employees of the Bell Telephone Company staying home with the flu on this date, the company took a half-page ad in many newspapers to tell Philadelphians that it could handle only "absolutely necessary calls compelled by the epidemic or by war necessity." Similar announcements were made in many municipalities that fall. The next day after the ad was run, the telephone company was authorized to cut off service to any persons making unessential calls, and the company ultimately did so in nearly a thousand cases.

October 10, 1918—To deal with both the telephone and the flu crisis in Philadelphia, on this date a bureau of information was opened in the Strawbridge and Clothier store mail-order department. There were 20 telephones answered 24 hours a day. Ads were placed in the newspapers telling people needing assistance to call "Filbert 100" and say "influenza." The bureau would attempt to supply doctors, nurses, ambulances, motor vehicles, or whatever as needed. A preliminary visit process was initiated to have volunteers visit to see what was really needed, and then the proper action would be taken. This process was estimated to save about one-third of the number of case referrals that otherwise would have been made to the overloaded medical organizations.

October 11, 1918 — More street activities were held in Philadelphia (and elsewhere in the region) because pledges were behind schedule for the Fourth Liberty Loan Drive, which was due to close on October 19. The Kaiser had sent messages on October 6 and 7 asking for a negotiated peace, but many felt this was just a ploy. They urged that the bond drive become a great success to demonstrate continuing resolve so that Germany could not win by negotiation what they could not win on the battlefield. So in spite of the flu danger, people turned out to push the bond drive over the top.

October 17, 1918 — On this date the last of the problems that armies of volunteers had helped solve was declared to be in hand. That problem was burying the dead. The city morgue was empty for the first time in many days, and the supply of available graves was catching up to demand, as were caskets. The number of dead from the flu/pneumonia would peak on the week ending October 19 and decline steadily thereafter.

The ban on church services was lifted on the 27th, and all other such bans were lifted by the 30th. Between September 29 and November 2, a period of about five weeks, 12,162 Philadelphians died. The flu epidemic process the city went through was similar to that of many other eastern seaboard cities. But at least there was no resurgence of flu later in the year and into 1919, as there was in many other places across the country. When the armistice came on November 11, 1918, to end the war, the flu epidemic also ended in Philadelphia.

October 19, 1918 — This was the effective date identified by Commissioner of Health J. W. Inches of Detroit, Michigan, on which Detroit would be declared off-limits to military personnel except those in perfect health on important military business and carrying a letter to that effect from a superior officer. The military was now being identified in many places as the prime carrier of the flu because of the many widely publicized outbreaks. Before this declaration could become an issue, Detroit was so badly infected by the flu that the attempt at a kind of reverse quarantine was quickly forgotten.

Actually, by this date flu deaths in the military had already peaked in the United Sates and were beginning to decline. The deaths among navy men ashore in the United States had peaked the week ending September 28, and deaths among army personnel had peaked the week ending October 11. Cities in the United States generally would reach their peaks in deaths in the week ending October 26, although several had a second, much smaller peak in January 1919.

October 26, 1918— On this date, Doctor William Hassler, chief of the San Francisco Board of Health, advised the citizens that the ordnance passed a week ago requiring the wearing of surgical-style masks would take a few days to establish a reduction in flu because of the incubation period of the flu. This ordnance began a comic-opera sequence about using such masks during the San Francisco flu epidemic. The masks could not stop the tiny flu virus from passing through, but the masks could stop droplets of water and dust particles possibly carrying the flu virus. However, to be effective they needed to be worn all the time. Further, wearing them outside where there was good ventilation was not really needed, but they could be effective when worn inside in close quarters. This was exactly the opposite of the way they were used in San Francisco.

Many smaller cities tried the masks in California, and in retrospect it was found that the masks made no difference in the rate and severity of the disease compared to cities where masks were not used. But in San Francisco, for reasons never explained, the use of the masks seemed to correlate with the fall of the flu.

October 27, 1918— As the flu/pneumonia epidemic of 1918 raged across the country, a Public Health Service reserve corps was established on this date to help meet the emergency.

November 21, 1918— The San Francisco Board of Health removed the ordnance requiring the wearing of surgical masks (*see entry for* October 26, 1918). Reported cases of the flu had peaked the week ending October 26, and the number of deaths reported had peaked the week after. These peaks seemed to coincide with the time when the number of persons wearing the masks had appeared to approach 100 percent of the population. By the end of November, new flu cases and reported deaths were back to the levels recorded at the beginning of October just before the epidemic began.

Dr. Hassler, the chief of the board of health, who had been the driving force behind the wearing of the masks, wanted their use to continue for a few more months. But wearing the masks had become somewhat of a joke. People began to slip them down under their chins or even wear them dangling from an ear. As the epidemic abated, the masks were considered too much of an inconvenience to be worthwhile. However, in San Francisco for some reason, when the masks officially came off, the rate of new cases of flu began to climb again. It was also climbing again in other California cities that had not made extensive use of the masks, but that was no consolation to San Francisco.

December 7, 1918— The mayor of San Francisco issued a proclamation suggesting that citizens of San Francisco begin wearing masks again as recommended by the board of health. The number of new flu cases was beginning to climb rapidly, but it was still well under the October levels. The citizens of San Francisco were not ready to wear masks again voluntarily, especially when many other health professionals were stating that the practice, as implemented in San Francisco, had very little effect on the spread of flu.

January 10, 1919— As new cases of the flu reached a level almost half that of the October 1918 peak (and deaths did the same), the San Francisco Board of Health voted to make the wearing of masks mandatory again. Amazingly, as soon as the ordnance went into effect on January 17, new flu cases almost immediately began to decline. However, San Franciscans, if they wore the masks at all, were seen again wearing them under their chin or dangling from an ear. It seemed as if the act of passing and repealing and passing the ordnance again was the thing that affected the flu statistics the most. On February 1, two weeks later, when new cases of the flu had fallen substantially, the board of health reversed the ordnance again and everyone could now legally stop wearing the masks. This time the rate of new flu cases continued to slowly decline, although it was spring before things roughly returned to normal.

April 3, 1919— The great flu pandemic of 1918–19 may have claimed one of its most crucial victims on this date, although no one was actually killed at the time. In the middle of negotiations trying to resolve the details of the peace to follow World War I, President Wilson of the United States started to develop a noticeably husky voice about three o'clock in the afternoon. By six o'clock he started to cough so convulsively he could hardly breathe. His temperature rose to 103 degrees, and he was so cramped with diarrhea he could hardly walk. The onset of the illness was so abrupt his doctor initially suspected poisoning. The assumption was that Wilson had caught the flu from French premier Clemenceau, who had had an explosive cough for some time.

President Wilson was not able to rejoin the talks until April 8, and by then he was no longer able to hold firm to his previous positions. The peace that emerged two months later was much different than that originally proposed by Wilson. Further, some analysts felt Wilson's stroke in September when he was trying without success to get the final settlement through Congress was partly a result of the illness Wilson had suffered in the spring. Wilson had never fully recovered from the flu.

May 1919— The *Journal of Industrial Hygiene* was established during this month. Until 1930, it remained the only American periodical in the field of occupational health. Other professional and educational efforts were made to help support the efforts of the journal, however, and occupational health became firmly established as a prime part of overall public health.

January 9, 1920— Charles-Edward Amory Winslow, professor of public health at Yale University, published an article titled "The Untilled Fields of Public Health." It was part of the ongoing discussion at the time of how far the jurisdiction of public health should reach compared to that of the basic medical profession and related institutions. Winslow felt, as did many leaders in the field, that public health should have a broad reach. His definition of public health, which was to cause some controversy, was: "the science and art of preventing disease, prolonging life, and promoting physical health and efficiency through organized community efforts for the sanitation of the environment, the control of community infections, the education of the individual in principles of personal hygiene, the organization of medical and nursing service for the early diagnosis and preventative treatment of disease, and the development of the social machinery which will insure to every individual in the community a standard of living adequate for the maintenance of health."

A broader mandate is hard to imagine, and the public health field would be embroiled in many battles about its mandate and the choices between focusing on environmental issues and individual issues. One analyst stated that in the sanitarian era before the twentieth century, public health was more concerned with engineering than medicine. But in the bacteriological era in the two decades around the turn of the century at 1900, public health concentrated on combating specific pathogenic organisms.

February 1920— This month generally is accepted as the end of the flu pandemic that ravaged the United States and the world during 1918 and 1919. The flu peaked in the United States from September through December of 1918, resurged at a lower lever in January of 1919 through the Spring of 1919, and then came back at an even lower lever into the beginning of 1920, after appearing to die out later in 1919. Although the epidemic was almost no longer noticeable in most of 1920, it caused enough deaths to make 1920 the year with the highest death rate from flu/pneumonia in the entire twentieth century in the United States except for 1918 and 1919.

After the epidemic, it was estimated that about one-quarter of the population of the United States, or 25 million people, caught the flu in 1918–19 and about 550,000 died. The number of deaths is probably even higher since not all areas were reliably reporting data at the time. The gross total may actually have approached 700,000. For comparison, the total number of battle deaths in World War I and II, the Korean War, and the Vietnam War adds up to 420,000. The flu epidemic of 1918–19 was a deadly event for the United States. Whether such an attack from our fellow travelers in the ocean of air in which we all live will ever occur again is impossible to tell.

August 1921— After an intensely active period of serving as assistant secretary of the navy under President Wilson, and then running for the vice-presidential nomination on the Democratic ticket in 1920 with James Cox, Franklin Delano Roosevelt was taking a break from politics at his family vacation home on Campobello Island off the coast of Maine. Even though he was 39 years old, he developed a case of polio that left his legs paralyzed for the rest of his life.

This was not only a personal tragedy for Roosevelt but potentially a professional one as well. Common wisdom said a crippled man could not expect to win high office in politics because he would be seen as weak. But Roosevelt turned that perception upside down. Instead he was perceived as a strong person who had overcome a great handicap and as a result had great empathy for others who were struggling. He went on to be elected governor of New York in 1928 and to be elected president of the United States in 1932 as the Great Depression was in its early stages and many people were in despair.

Roosevelt never stopped looking for a cure that would permit him to walk again. In 1924, he tried a resort in Warm Springs, Georgia, whose waters were said by a friend to have curative powers. Roosevelt stayed there for a time then decided to buy the run-down resort in 1926 and try to operate it as a rehabilitation center for polio victims, including himself. It was the beginning of a process that would lead to the famous March of Dimes in 1938 and on to the Salk vaccine against polio in 1954.

September 20, 1921— The Public Health Service (PHS) established the Rocky Mountain Spotted Fever Laboratory on this date in a former school building in Hamilton, Montana. It was recognized as an official PHS field station.

December 6, 1921— On this date the United States Public Health Service (PHS) began weekly health broadcasts from the naval observatory station in Arlington, Virginia. This was an attempt to take advantage of the radio craze that had developed in the United States during the past year. Dr. Charles A. Powers, President of the American Society for the Control of Cancer, made the first such broadcast in the previous month. Three months later, on March 24, 1922, the New York State Health Department gave a talk on "Keeping Well" from the General Electric station in Schenectady, New York. Radio had been added to the methods of disseminating public health information, and television would follow in its time about two decades later.

August 1, 1922 — A Special Cancer Investigations Laboratory was established on this date at Harvard University by Public Health Service investigators.

February 1923 — In the American Medical Association (AMA) Bulletin No. 16 issued during this month, it was reported by the medical director of a region in Ohio that a recent program to give individual health examinations had been very successful. About 90 percent of the people found to have medical problems had asked for follow-up treatment, and neighbors, friends, and relatives had applied for complete physical examinations in record numbers.

This trend towards individual medical examinations had been given a boost by the creation of the Life Extension Institute in 1914. The institute was associated with life insurance companies, and it began offering checkups through boards of physicians around the country. The results of screening recruits for World War I showed that the overwhelming majority had medical issues. Other experimental mass screenings showed the same high percentages of medical problems, many of which were preventable. Thus, in this era, the concept of mass screening for diseases as a key part of public health programs was established.

January 19, 1929 — The Narcotics Control Act provided for construction of two hospitals for the care and treatment of drug addicts, and authorized the creation of a narcotics division in the Public Health Service's office of the surgeon general. Many people would be surprised to learn how long today's highly publicized problem of drug addiction has been with us.

May 1929 — Alexander Fleming this month published the results of his work over the past year with penicillin. With his limited facilities he was unable to do more than make very small amounts of penicillin, and he published his results in the hope that someone would take up his work at the point where he was forced to stop. As described in the introduction in "The Coming of Chemotherapy and Antibiotics," Fleming was not contacted until near the end of the 1930s, but he had kept alive a sample of penicillin for a decade by transferring it from one petri dish to another. This sample led to the mass production of penicillin that saved the lives of many wounded soldiers in World War II. Penicillin and its derivatives became the most famous and most widely used of the antibiotics, and Fleming shared the Nobel Prize in 1945 for his part in its development.

April 9, 1930—A law changed the name of the Advisory Board of the Hygienic Laboratory within the Public Health Service to the National Advisory Health Council. The Hygenic Laboratory would soon become the National Institute of Health (*see next entry*).

May 26, 1930—The Ransdell Act expanded and reorganized the Hygienic Laboratory of the Public Health Service and renamed it the National Institute of Health (NIH). The Act provided $750,000 for the construction of two buildings for the NIH and authorized a system of fellowships. This was the start of many decades of NIH funded research into so many areas that the National Institute of Health would become the National Institutes of Health.

June 14, 1930—A law created a separate Bureau of Narcotics in the Treasury Department to control trading in narcotic drugs and their use for therapeutic purposes. The Narcotics Division within the Public Health Service (*see entry for* January 29, 1929) was redesignated as the Division of Mental Hygiene. This authorized the surgeon general to investigate the abuse of narcotics and the causes, treatment, and prevention of nervous and mental diseases.

November 1933—A meeting was held in Warm Springs, Georgia, to plan methods of raising funds for President Roosevelt's polio rehabilitation center there. Basil O'Connor, once the president's law partner, was in charge of the Warm Springs operation as President Roosevelt had requested back in 1928 when Roosevelt was elected governor of New York. O'Connor, realizing the resort bought by Roosevelt in 1926 (*see entry for* August 1921) could not succeed financially on its own, had previously incorporated it as a foundation eligible to receive donations. Warm Springs had grown, made many improvements, and was helping a number of polio patients but competition was tight for funds. At the time, there were over 75 other groups formed to raise funds for specific diseases.

The key to fund-raising for polio was the immense popularity of the president. In a way that could not be done today, James Farley, close friend of the president and also postmaster general of the United States, organized the postmasters across the United States to host a birthday ball for the president's birthday on January 30, 1934. Six thousand events were arranged, including an opulent gala at the Waldorf-Astoria in New York attended by the president's mother. President Roosevelt made a radio address to welcome the partygoers, and the first series of the officially titled Celebration Balls in Honor of the President's Birthday were a major success. The events cleared a profit of over $1 million, over ten times what was anticipated.

The decision was easily made to make the balls an annual event. But much more importantly, the amount of money raised this time established the thought that eventually enough money could be raised to continue the work of helping polio patients and also fund research projects to find a way to eliminate the disease. Thus began a private fund-raising effort that would directly improve public health in terms of assistance to polio patients (including the purchase of crutches, wheelchairs and iron lungs) and would ultimately lead to a vaccine to protect against the disease.

June 8, 1934—President Roosevelt, in a special message to Congress on this date, announced he was seeking "sound means" to provide more security for the common man. This action was to lead to the Social Security Act in another year, but discussions on health insurance that were a part of the review process did not lead to a specific national health insurance policy. Still, this was the real first shot in a battle that was to continue for the rest of the twentieth century and into today.

August 14, 1935—The Social Security Act enacted on this date was much more than an act to provide payments to citizens in retirement. It also authorized health grants to the states on the basis that the most effective way to prevent the interstate spread of disease was to improve state and local public health programs. In this way, the U.S. Public Health Service became an advisor and practical assistant to state and local health services.

August 15, 1935—The edition of the *New York State Journal of Medicine* published on this date contained a paper published by doctors Maurice Brodie and William Park, and one by and Dr. Park alone (Park was known as the conqueror of diphtheria) that essentially claimed a vaccine for polio had been developed. But the papers were inaccurate in that they claimed there was only one basic type of poliovirus (we now know there are three). The tests of the vaccine from Park and Brodie and an associated vaccine produced by Doctor John A. Kolmer actually produced some paralytic polio and deaths. An investigation by Dr. James P. Leake of the Public Health Service of the two vaccines showed that the vaccines should be withdrawn. Both were in fact withdrawn following a meeting of the American Public Health Association at St. Louis in November 1935 at which Dr. Leake presented the results of his investigation. The false start on the polio vaccines had a dampening effect on work in the field until Dr. Jonas Salk successfully developed a vaccine that worked in the early 1950s.

July 1936— A school health education study was launched in New York City under the direction of Dorothy B. Nyswander. This study focused on the best way to administer and practice public health in schools and was published in 1942 as *Solving School Health Problems.* New York City had been a leader in this field for most of the twentieth century to this date, and much of what was decided in this four-year study influenced health actions for school children for decades to come. Greater emphasis was placed on more thorough, if less frequent, medical examinations by the family or school physician. The key need, as it almost always had been, was for follow-up activities to be sure that problems that were uncovered resulted in some action, especially among students who do not have easy access to medical care.

February 1, 1937— Dr. Lewis R. Thompson was appointed director of the National Institute of Health (NIH) within the Public Health Service, and the NIH was reorganized into eight divisions. These divisions focused on specific diseases, and they would form the basis for a future reorganization into the National Institutes of Health.

August 5, 1937— The National Cancer Institute was created on this date (following the signing of a law two weeks earlier) to conduct and support research into the cause, diagnosis, and treatment of cancer. The surgeon general of the Public Health Service was authorized to make grants, provide fellowships, train personnel, and assist the states in their efforts against cancer.

September 23, 1937— President Roosevelt announced the formation of the National Foundation for Infantile Paralysis (NFIP). The foundation was incorporated the following January 1938. Basil O'Connor was appointed the president of the foundation but continued his work with the Warm Springs operation (*see entry for* November 1933).

Basil O'Connor had recommended this move to Roosevelt to refocus the donations made at the President's birthday balls for the battle on polio. President Roosevelt had many more critics now, and the donations raised at the birthday balls were steadily declining. Now it was time to focus on the other victims of polio, especially crippled children. Hence the use of an official name for the disease, Infantile Paralysis. Hollywood studios, who were under anti-trust threats in the mid–1930s, had previously shown a strong interest in having their stars become associated with the fund-raising efforts via the

Presidential birthday balls. Now that the focus was on crippled children, many stars wanted to get involved on their own.

Eddie Cantor, a long-time movie comedian now with a popular radio program, later suggested that he and several others use their programs to urge people to contribute to the new charity when it was launched in January 1938 near the time the president's normal birthday balls (some of which were still being held) would take place. Cantor also suggested using the theme of the March of Dimes for the new cause, taking off on the title of the popular newsreel feature, the "March of Time." Cantor was already an experienced fund-raiser for Jewish charities, and he understood the power radio had to move people.

January 1938—The first appeal for the March of Dimes aired during the last week of this month (*see entry for* September 23, 1937). In addition to the Eddie Cantor show, the Lone Ranger radio program also made an appeal that week for kids to send dimes to the president to conquer the disease that had crippled so many of their playmates. Two days after Cantor's broadcast, the normal White House daily mail of 5,000 letters grew to 30,000. The next day it was 50,000, and the day after that 150,000. Fifty extra postal clerks were hired, and they still couldn't keep up with the deluge. The new foundation ultimately raised $1.8 million, including $268,000 received in the form of 2.68 million dimes.

The March of Dimes was a great success, and movie stars stayed involved with its fund-raising. To ease the strain on the White House mail, the collection of dimes moved from the mail to movie houses, where ushers passed through with collection baskets or coin containers after a movie star appeared in a short film clip urging donations. Now that funds were available in regular sizeable amounts, research programs were initiated that would result in a vaccine in just 15 years, in spite of the impact of World War II. The March of Dimes was on the march, supported in part by countless women volunteers who took up the slack when many men were drafted for the war.

July 1938—The National Institute of Health (NIH) moved to Bethesda, Maryland, during this month. There were multiple gifts of land made during the year to the NIH by Mrs. Luke I. Wilson, and Congress approved construction of new, larger laboratory facilities. The Bethesda address became familiar to most Americans in countless press releases and information requests during the rest of the century.

April 3, 1939—The Reorganization Act of 1939 transferred the Public Health Service (PHS) from the Treasury Department, where the PHS had been since it was created in 1798, to the newly created Federal Security Agency

(FSA). This new agency was meant to bring together federal programs related to personal security such as health and social welfare including education, social security, and the PHS. The new agency had nothing to do with national security in the sense we know it today. The FSA would soon be reorganized again, and eventually became the Department of Health, Education, and Welfare in 1953.

May 1939— A Food Stamp Plan was inaugurated to supply families on relief and those having low incomes with food at public expense through local outlets. This plan was operated in conjunction with plans to provide free school lunches and "the removal of agricultural surpluses."

October 31, 1940— President Roosevelt took part in a dedication ceremony for the new buildings and grounds of the National Institute of Health (NIH). By 1942 Mrs. Luke Wilson had donated a total of 92 acres of ground in Bethesda, Maryland, to the NIH. These donations formed the core of what, with later land purchases by the federal government, became the 306.4-acre reservation of the NIH that still exists today.

January 18, 1943— War Food Order No. 1 went into effect on this date. The order required that white bread be enriched with niacin, riboflavin, thiamine, and iron. While this policy remained in effect only until the end of the war, many states continued it on their own and enriched products became generally common in the marketplace.

May 1943— Avery Oswald, who had worked tirelessly at the Rockefeller Institute for over three decades on problems involved with pneumonia, told his brother on this day that he had determined that the element called by scientists the "transforming principle" up to that time was actually DNA, the acid at the heart of heredity in organisms, including humans. Avery and others published their findings in 1944. Almost a decade later in April 1953, James Watson and Francis Crick would announce their determination of the famous double-helix nature of DNA.

December 1943— As the German Army left Naples, Italy, a typhus epidemic was just beginning. A typhus team was sent to Naples to try to break the epidemic before Allied soldiers entered Naples. The team was using a new chemical called DDT that had just been successfully tested as a possible pesticide by the United States Department of Agriculture in Orlando, Florida, after being developed by the J. R. Geigy Company in Switzerland. Typhus was spread by lice, and DDT, in addition to being a ferocious killer of mosquitoes, seemed to be a magic killer of all sorts of pests. The DDT proved to be miraculous in Naples as well, and the typhus epidemic was over before the Allied troops arrived. DDT would start out as heroic, but in two decades it would become a problem exactly because it killed such a wide range of things (but not humans) and stayed in the environment for a very long time.

In 1947, after World War II, DDT would be used to clear the Island of Sardinia, often thought to be the most malarious part of Italy. The mosquito-causing malaria was thoroughly routed. There were 75,000 cases of malaria on the island in 1946 but only nine by 1951. Thoughts were given to eradicating malaria, a deadly killer in many areas, from the world. It would almost happen, but eradication needed to be done completely in a timely manner before the remaining mosquitoes could develop resistance to DDT. It was difficult to get 100 percent eradication in many areas (although it happened in some).

Then, in 1962, Rachael Carson published *Silent Spring*, pointing out that DDT killed many things (including prior predators of mosquitoes that were gone if the mosquitoes returned, leaving you worse off than ever), and that it stayed in the environment and continue to cause unintended havoc. Eventually, DDT was banned by all nations but India and China, who decided the trade-off in the elimination of malaria deaths was worth the other risks (*Silent Spring* did not mention that about 10 million lives had been saved by DDT in the two decades prior to the book's publication). There are few simple solutions in the area of public health anywhere in the world.

July 1, 1944 — The Public Health Service Act divided the U.S. Public Health Service into the Office of the Surgeon General, the Bureau of Medical Services, the Bureau of State Services, and the National Institute of Health (NIH). The act gave the surgeon general broader powers and made the National Cancer Institute a division of the NIH. The act also established a clinical center within the PHS to study certain patients and empowered the PHS to eventually create the Research Grant Office on January 1, 1946; the Experimental Biology and Medicine Institute and the National Microbiological Institute on November 1, 1948; and the Division of Research Services on January 1, 1956. This act made the PHS a formidable national force in directing nearly everything having to do with public health.

November 10, 1944 — Wolfgang A. Casper, a 43-year-old naturalized doctor from Germany who had fled Hitler and his attacks on Jews, came to the podium at a conference on venereal disease control. Casper had agreed to join the Public Health Service (PHS) in the United States for the duration of the war, but he was internationally known for his work on a possible vaccine against gonorrhea, the most prevalent of the venereal diseases that included syphilis. But Casper had hardly begun speaking before Dr. J. R. Heller, a doctor who outranked Casper within the Public Health Service, interrupted him. Dr. Heller said there would no need for a vaccine now that the new Sulfa drugs and penicillin were available and could be made at low cost to eradicate any cases of gonorrhea and syphilis. Casper protested that the diseases would outlive them both, but he was overruled.

This was a classical example of the misunderstanding of the use of antibiotics when they first appeared. The new drugs would certainly cure the diseases by destroying the germs that caused them, but the new drugs could not prevent new cases. The number of new cases that would occur in the future in diseases of this type would mean that the diseases would always be with us. And so they are, in far greater numbers than ever. The new antibiotic drugs would hopefully stop the diseases from being fatal if cures were sought in time, but the fact that preventing new cases of a disease with an appropriate vaccination is far better than trying to cure them after they have occurred has been proven repeatedly.

November 20, 1944— The antibiotic streptomycin was administered for the first time to a critically ill tuberculosis patient. The result was essentially miraculous. The disease was quickly arrested, the bacteria that cause tuberculosis disappeared from his sputum, and the patient made a rapid recovery. Finally, one of mankind's biggest killers was capable of being stopped by an antibiotic drug.

Streptomycin was developed by Selman A. Waksman, a soil biology expert. He knew that the recently developed penicillin was not effective against such bacteria as the kind that causes tuberculosis, and he also knew from long study that tuberculosis bacteria do not survive in soil. By constant experimentation he found the element in soil that destroys tuberculosis bacteria (as in the case of penicillin, it was a type of mold), and streptomycin was the ultimate result. Waksman developed a number of related drugs after coming up with streptomycin, and he was eventually awarded the Nobel Prize in 1952.

June 1946— The Food and Drug Administration (FDA) was transferred from the Department of Agriculture to the new Federal Security Agency (FSA). The FSA gave way to Health, Education, and Welfare (HEW) in 1953, and the FDA became a division of the Public Health Service (PHS) in 1968, after the PHS and FDA were made part of HEW in 1953.

July 3, 1946— The National Mental Health Act was created to provide research into the causes, diagnosis, and treatment of psychiatric disorders. Again, the surgeon general was designated to provide support to state mental health programs. Accordingly, the National Institute of Mental Health was established on April 15, 1949.

March 1948 — Doctor John Enders and his team at the Boston Children's Hospital succeed in growing the virus that causes mumps in chicken tissue cultures. Being able to grow a virus in a convenient culture and being able to cause appropriate infections afterwards is a key step in producing a vaccine. In a next step, the team tried to grow poliovirus in a non-nervous system human cell culture and became the first group in history to succeed. Before then it was thought that the poliovirus would grow only in human nervous system tissue. It was widely known a vaccine could not be made from such tissue because it could cause deadly allergic reactions in the brain when it was injected.

Enders made one additional breakthrough when he showed that the effects of the virus acting on human cells could be clearly seen through a regular microscope even if the virus itself could not be seen. This made it possible to grow the poliovirus easily and then check for essentially an immune reaction without using large numbers of monkeys as test animals and then waiting to see how they responded to subsequent injections with different types of poliovirus. This part of the work was supported by the March of Dimes, which was trying to confirm that there were only three types of poliovirus. Enders gave them a much quicker way to confirm this fact and to develop a vaccine and subsequently test it against the three confirmed types that existed. Enders and his team won a Noble Prize in 1954 for their work.

June 16, 1948 — The National Heart Act authorized the National Heart Institute to conduct, assist, and foster research; provide training; and assist the states in the prevention, diagnosis, and treatment of heart diseases. The name of the National Institute of Health was officially changed to the National Institutes of Health to recognize that the activities at the institute were being broadened to cover a wider range of diseases being covered in more depth.

June 24, 1948 — The National Dental Research Act authorized the National Institute of Dental Research to perform the same functions for dental disease as had been authorized for heart disease just eight days earlier. No profession wanted to be left out.

November 1, 1948 — The National Microbiological Institute and the Experimental Biology and Medicine Institute were formed within the National Institutes of Health. At the same time, the already existing Rocky Mountain Laboratory and Biologics Control Laboratory became part of the National Microbiological Institute.

January 1950— Doctor Jonas Salk, a 36-year-old doctor who had chosen to do medical research rather than pursue public practice, started tissue-culture production of the poliovirus. Salk had come to work at the less-prestigious University of Pittsburgh medical program because he was promised the facilities to run a research program as the city of Pittsburgh tried to upgrade its image from that of a smoke-filled steel-manufacturing city. In order to help fund his laboratory facilities, Salk had accepted a grant from the March of Dimes to take part in a program to confirm that there were only three types of poliovirus. The tedious work demanded caring for and feeding many monkeys, who besides man and chimpanzees were among the few species that got polio. But Salk immediately picked up on the work done by John Enders (*see entry for* March 1948) and began to complete the process much more rapidly using human tissue cultures.

    Salk had decided to pursue a polio vaccine using killed poliovirus. This was inherently safer than a weakened live virus vaccine, but many researchers felt it would provide only temporary immunity. A weakened live virus vaccine had the statistical risk that some viruses would not be weakened enough and would produce a full-blown case of polio. Doctors in favor of the live-virus approach felt a good vaccine was still 15 years off, and they came to resent the speed with which Salk and his March of Dimes backers wanted to move. They felt there was too much inaccurate publicity about the killed virus approach and its promise of a polio vaccine in just a few years. But Salk was far ahead of everyone else and determined to move ahead with his plans.

August 15, 1950— The Omnibus Medical Research Act authorized the surgeon general to create the National Institute of Neurological Diseases and Blindness as well as additional institutes for other specified diseases. These other diseases included arthritis and metabolic diseases and allergy and infectious diseases. The Public Health Service was now involved in nearly every major disease or disease process occurring in the United States.

May 23, 1952— With the poliovirus typing program complete and confirming that there were indeed only three types of poliovirus (*see entry for* January 1950), Jonas Salk was ready to begin initial testing of his vaccine. On this day, he drove 80 miles to the Polk State School for retarded males, both adults and children. Members of an institution were ideal for such experiments because they were in isolated circumstances. Their diets and other aspects of their lives were closely controlled, they were available for repeated tests, and accurate records could be kept.

    It should be noted that Salk's work posed no risk to the people being tested. Since it was a killed-virus vaccine, no on could get polio from it. Salk had already tested it on himself and his family and a number of volunteers at his laboratory to be sure there were no unexpected side effects. Salk was simply taking blood samples before and after the injection of the vaccine to confirm that the persons receiving the vaccine were creating the antibodies needed to defeat a naturally occurring poliovirus.

In addition to the Polk State School, Salk was also testing children at the Watson Home for Crippled Children. This home contained children who had already been crippled by polio, and Salk hoped to show that his vaccine would create more antibodies against polio than the real thing had been able to do. The Watson home was much closer to Pittsburgh, and the atmosphere was much more pleasant than the one at the Polk State School. The crippled children at Watson came to love Dr. Salk, who had a very pleasant bedside manner and who always brought lots of lollipops to distribute with his shots and blood tests. Salk kept his tests going through the summer of 1952. No one got ill in any way, and the tests proved that Salk's vaccine increased antibodies in a way that should protect against polio.

January 1, 1953—As of this date, about 59 percent of the civilian population of the United States had hospitalization insurance of some kind. This was a dramatic increase over the about 2,000 people enrolled in the one Blue Cross plan that was available in 1933.

Blue Cross had developed out of a Baylor University plan initially offered in 1929 in Dallas. The "Baylor Plan" was developed by a Baylor official named Justin Ford Kimball. The plan guaranteed schoolteachers 21 days of hospital care at the Baylor University Hospital for a payment of six dollars a year (collected on the basis of 50 cents a month). The primary idea was to have coverage for the near-inevitable event of childbirth, but other needs were also covered. However, the plan was restricted to the use of the Baylor hospital. Other plans soon developed that permitted use of other hospitals, and this was the beginning of what we now know as Blue Cross.

The Blue Shield medical insurance plan grew out of lumber and mining camps of the Pacific Northwest around the turn of the century. Employees wanted to provide medical care for their employees, and they did so via medical service bureaus composed of physicians to whom the employers paid a fee. This led to the founding of the Blue Shield plan in California in 1939.

The Blue Cross symbol was well established by 1939, and the Blue Shield symbol was well established by 1948. The two plans merged in 1982. Although the two plans kept growing, the issue of whether the federal government should offer national health insurance (as it essentially does to those over 65 via Medicare) continues to be debated.

January 23, 1953—At a two-day meeting of the immunization committee of the National Foundation for Infantile Paralysis (NFIP) in Hershey,

Pennsylvania, the committee learned for the first time of Salk's work in the field that had taken place during the summer of 1952. Dr. Albert Sabin counseled patience and suggested the development of an effective polio vaccine could take another 10–15 years. But a majority voted to plan to arrange a field trial in the near future. However, in retrospect it was clear that the scientists, like Doctor Sabin, were intending only to think about moving ahead with a field trial, with the date and the vaccine to be tried yet to be determined. But the NFIP members intended to go ahead with a massive field trial as soon as possible, using the polio vaccine that had been developed and tested on a limited scale by Doctor Salk. Basil O'Connor, head of the NFIP, continually stressed the number of children that would be crippled while waiting for a more "prudent" course to be taken. O'Connor felt that maybe Salk did not have *the* vaccine, but he had *a* vaccine that appeared to work. The vote to proceed, which soon caused headlines around the world, was a first step to the highly publicized (and highly successful) field trials using Salk's vaccine that would take place in the spring of 1954.

March 28, 1953— Dr. Jonas Salk published a formal paper in the *Journal of the American Medical Association* titled "Studies in Human Subjects on Active Immunization Against Poliomyelitis." It was basically an elaboration of the report he had given to the immunization committee on January 23, 1953. Now more pressure began to build for a full-scale field test of Salk's vaccine.

April 11, 1953— Under the new president, Dwight Eisenhower, a major reorganization took place in the area of public health. A new cabinet-level department was created called the Department of Health, Education, and Welfare (HEW). The Public Health Service (PHS) was assigned to the department with the Food and Drug Administration (FDA). Eventually, in 1968, the FDA would become a division of the PHS. When the Department of Education was formed in 1979, HEW became the Department of Health and Human Services, officially making its debut under this name on May 4, 1980.

June 22, 1953— Dr. Jonas Salk met alone with Basil O'Connor, head of the National Foundation for Infantile Paralysis, to agree on a date when a national field trial of Salk's polio vaccine could begin. They agreed to begin a trial before the 1954 polio season, which would be early in the spring of 1954. Meanwhile, in the spring of 1953, before his meeting with O'Connor, Salk had already vaccinated some 600 additional people in the Pittsburgh area, many of whom were anxious to gain some potential protection against polio for the 1953 polio season.

July 15, 1953—In the publication *California's Health* carrying this date, it was pointed out that the California State Board of Education was employing more public health nurses than the state board of health. This was an example of a big discussion of the time that public health administration among the cities and the states was getting more and more fragmented. Whereas before the New Deal of the 1930s, many efforts had to be made to create boards of health in the states and the cities, the emphasis on social welfare in the 1930s had resulted in multiple organizations dealing with some aspect of health care after World War II. One result was to draw the federal government even further into public health activities to coordinate what was going on across the nation.

October 24, 1953—The Immunization Committee of the National Foundation for Infantile Paralysis (NFIP) met in Detroit for the first time since the January 23–24 meeting in Hershey, Pennsylvania. Many of the scientists came prepared to discuss alternative vaccines to try in a yet-to-be determined time frame for a field test. But Basil O'Connor, head of the NFIP, decided it was time to make clear the distinction he felt existed between the committee's function to advise about the field trial as opposed to direct the field trial, which the scientists felt they should do. When the question was asked about determining which vaccine(s) to try and when, O'Connor replied sharply that such decisions "were not the function of this committee."

There was an immediate breach between the committee and the NFIP. Some scientists tried to get the National Institutes of Health (NIH) under the government's Public Health Service to take over the funding of their research rather than the NFIP. Many spoke out against O'Connor's plans for a field trial of Salk's vaccine as soon as possible. But O'Connor was not deterred. He wanted to stop polio without waiting years for a more traditional scientific approach. From this date onward, he and Salk would be under attack by the scientific community at large, an attack that would not end until April 1955 when the results of the 1954 field trial showed Salk's vaccine to be a great success. But even then resentment would linger against Salk, and some felt this resentment was a factor in Salk's failure to win a Nobel Prize for his triumph over polio.

November 11, 1953—Basil O'Connor, head of the National Foundation for Infantile Paralysis (NFIP), met in New York with the top executives of America's leading pharmaceutical companies to discuss production of polio vaccine for the coming 1954 field trial. The only company at the meeting already planning to make vaccine for the trial was Parke Davis, with whom Jonas Salk was having ongoing battles about methods of production. Other companies willing and able to take part were Eli Lilly and Company, the

Pitman-Moore Company, Sharpe and Dhome, Wyeth Laboratories, and Cutter Laboratories.

The companies were interested because it was clear that a successful field trial would produce an instant market for the product. Further, participation in the field trial would give a company a good start in supplying the follow-on market. But a field-trial failure would mean a lot of work for nothing. O'Connor eventually had to guarantee to buy large quantities of the vaccine regardless of the field trial results to get more companies to participate. However, this gamble paid off handsomely when the field trial succeeded and initially there was not enough vaccine available to meet the sudden immense demand.

December 5, 1953 — On this date Basil O'Connor, the head of the National Foundation for Infantile Paralysis, and one of the foundation's chief executive doctors, Hart Van Ripper, met in New York with Thomas Francis Jr., a very well known and respected physician and virologist who was also the director of the School of Public Health at the University of Michigan. Ironically, Jonas Salk had begun his career studying under Francis at the University of Michigan in the early 1940s. The meeting with Francis followed an urgent transatlantic call (a rarity in those days) to reach Francis on a sabbatical in Europe to convince him to administer the field trial of the Salk vaccine in the spring of 1954.

This was a stroke of genius in many ways by O'Connor. Francis was so highly respected in the field of virology that even the scientists who were angry at O'Connor and Salk for going out on their own agreed that any field trial administered by Thomas Francis was unquestionably well designed and its results would be highly credible. Further, Jonas Salk, who felt constantly under attack and was stretched quite thin trying to manage the field trial and oversee the production of the vaccine at Parke-Davis and still run his own laboratory, would get a large weight removed from his shoulders by a man he trusted implicitly. Salk was opposed to a double-blind field trial that would result in the highest scientific credibility because he wanted any child who agreed to take part in the trial to get his vaccine and not a placebo, but he immediately agreed to Francis' insistence on a mostly double blind approach. Salk, who felt he needed to be in charge of every aspect of the field trail to be sure it was done right, was glad to give the responsibility for actually designing the field trial and interpreting its results to Francis.

Francis was not sure he wanted the job. He could see accurately the problems that were involved, especially with many scientists angry about O'Connor's and Salk's determination to plow ahead on their own to get a vaccine against polio in the shortest possible time, instead of listening to the advice of the scientists who knew better and urged a more leisurely and careful course. But Francis took the job because he felt it was the right thing to do and he felt indebted to the National Foundation for Infantile Paralysis for their support of his facilities at the University of Michigan over the years. Francis was frankly annoyed at the other scientists who were upset that they were not in charge of the effort. Without the work of Thomas Francis, the field trial would have been delayed at least a year and another round of children would have been crippled by polio, which had its largest epidemic ever in the United States in 1952.

January 25, 1954— After much discussion, Thomas Francis completed in writing the plan for the field trial of the Salk polio vaccine. If they wanted to do it before the 1954 polio season began, everything would have to be in place and ready to go in almost exactly three months. There was a lot of work to do, but at least there was a plan for everyone to follow, and for the first time for many of them it appeared that the field trial would actually take place.

February 1954— The National Foundation for Infantile Paralysis (NFIP) abandoned its exclusive contract with Parke-Davis to produce the vaccine for the upcoming field trial of Jonas Salk's polio vaccine and invited other companies to take part. They might not have large quantities of vaccine available for the field trial (only Parke-Davis and Eli Lilly actually did so), but at least they would be ready for the follow up. The move to break the Parke-Davis monopoly greatly pleased Jonas Salk, who felt competition would force the companies to follow a single set of specifications as approved by him. Salk felt Parke-Davis was trying to employ techniques it preferred even if they did not meet Salk's approval. Six companies agreed to take part, but to give them an incentive Basil O'Connor, head of NFIP, agreed to buy all of the entire first year's output of the vaccine, even if the field trial were not successful. This was a $9 million gamble by O'Connor that paid off very well in 1955.

March 11, 1954— After meetings with federal and state officials and executives of the National Foundation for Infantile Paralysis, a date of April 19, 1954, was set for the beginning of the national field trial for the Salk polio vaccine. Safety concerns required Salk to vaccinate successfully another 5,000 children in the Pittsburgh area, but the last hurdle to the field trial seemed to have been overcome.

April 4, 1954— Walter Winchell, a trendy gossip columnist of the time who was in decline, went on radio to claim that the Salk vaccine had been implicated in several animal deaths and that the National Foundation for

Infantile Paralysis (NFIP) had prepared a number of "little white coffins" for the children who would die in the upcoming field trial. Winchell typically refused to name his source for this false information, but analysts suspected it was Paul de Kruif, a once-popular science writer who harbored a grudge against Basil O'Connor of the NFIP. Winchell's ridiculous charges were quickly refuted by the NFIP, and several state local medical associations that said they would withdraw from the field trial found themselves under attack from furious parents who did not want their children to miss the chance to take part. By the time the field trials started with a one-week delay on April 26, most of those state local associations had requested to be put back in the field trials.

April 26, 1954— The first of some 650,000 children vaccinated in the field trial of the Salk polio vaccine received the first of their series of shots on this morning. The first child to be vaccinated and photographed as a "Polio Pioneer" was six-year-old Randy Kerr of McLean, Virginia. He would attend the 25th anniversary of the 1955 report on the results of the field trial in 1980, when he was taller than Dr. Salk and polio was mostly a memory.

Including the children who did not receive a real polio vaccination or any shot at all and were acting as controls, about 1.8 million children took part in the field trial. It was the most massive event of its type up to that time, and it was entirely privately funded, primarily by the successful campaigns of the March of Dimes since 1938. It was the prime public health event of the 1900s in the United States, and about the only thing everyone involved in public health agrees about is that something like it could never happen in today's litigious atmosphere.

There was one amusing circumstance showing that many people felt the vaccine would work well before any results of the tests were in. There was pilferage of the vaccine by people, including doctors, who took it home for distribution to children not in the field trial and to various friends and neighbors. They did not want to get polio while waiting for the test results, and the general distribution of the vaccine that would follow in the next year if the field trials were successful.

June 1954— By the end of this month, the last of the vaccinations had been given for the field trial of the Salk polio vaccine (there was a series of three shots). All of the data was being assembled and shipped to Ann Arbor, Michigan, where Thomas Francis had established his data evaluation unit at the University of Michigan. Security was tight and there were no leaks. No one, including Dr. Salk himself, would discover the results of the field trial until they were publicly announced in April 1955.

December 1954— Even before the results of the field trial of the Salk polio vaccine were in, the National Foundation for Infantile Paralysis (NFIP) gave Doctor Albert Sabin a sizeable grant to further develop his live-virus polio vaccine. The general scientific community felt Sabin's vaccine would give longer immunity than the killed-virus Salk vaccine. During the next decade the NFIP would give Rubin almost two million dollars to support his work. However, Sabin would initially have to look abroad to find places to mass test his vaccine. The Salk vaccine would prove to work quite well enough for most in its initial series of tests.

March 9, 1955— The last delinquent data was finally received at the evaluation center for the 1954 field trial tests of the Salk polio vaccine. A planned announcement date was being seriously discussed, because there had to be enough time to get the vaccine out for the 1955 polio season if it proved successful. That meant the announcement of the results had to take place no later than mid–April. Further, several media groups that planned to be present for the announcement, including Edward R. Murrow and his famous *See It Now* program which had done an initial program on Jonas Salk on February 22, 1955, wanted the announcement to be made on a Tuesday for programming reasons. The announcement date was set for Tuesday, April 12, 1955, to meet all these requirements. Then it was realized that this date was the 10th anniversary of the death of President Franklin Roosevelt. It was decided to be an appropriate choice. In another coincidence that almost no one noticed, April 12, 1955, was also the 13th anniversary of the day a young Jonas Salk had begun his work in the field of virology under Thomas Francis at the University of Michigan in 1942.

April 1, 1955— The Cancer Chemotherapy National Service Center was established to coordinate the first national cancer chemotherapy program. The treatment of cancer continued to gain new focus as cancer death rates in the United States continued to steadily increase.

April 12, 1955— Amid a huge media frenzy, the Salk polio vaccine field trial of 1954 was pronounced a great success. The results were far better than anyone had hoped, and Jonas Salk became a celebrity of the first rank around the world. The Department of Health, Education, and Welfare had scientists on hand at the meeting so it could license the vaccine as "safe and effective" before the day was over. Plans were made for mass vaccinations to begin as soon as possible.

    Almost immediately, problems began with the production and allocation of the vaccine. Countries outside the United States also clamored for the vaccine, and the never-subtle hand of international politics soon was involved in the mix. But these problems were still some time away. Nothing could dampen the joy of this day for Jonas Salk, who stood vindicated, along with Basil O'Connor of the National Institute for Infantile Paralysis, for taking an independent — and faster — route to find a vaccine that would stop polio. Letters of thanks, most including money, poured into the Salk laboratory and home in Pittsburgh. Better yet, Salk knew the rare pleasure of standing up to those who "knew better" and being proven right.

April 22, 1955—Jonas Salk received a special citation from President Eisenhower at the White House for Salk's work in developing the polio vaccine. It was one of the few rewards and honors heaped on Salk after April 12, that Salk, a relatively private man, attended in person.

April 26, 1955—After two weeks of great news on the polio front, word came that children in Idaho and California were getting polio from the polio vaccine. This potentially disastrous news turned out to be the result of one company, Cutter Laboratories in Berkeley, California, turning out some bad batches of the vaccine due to production errors. After an investigation headed by Leonard Scheele, the surgeon general of the United States, the problem was basically isolated and in retrospect turned out to be limited. But Cutter had clearly comprised production safety and would have to eventually pay victims in court, and there were many complaints about normal government doublespeak that made it hard to find out exactly what was going on. The other vaccine production companies made some extra safety checks and polio vaccine production resumed reasonably quickly.

May 19, 1955—In the middle of ongoing disputes over the production and allocation of the Salk polio vaccine, Oveta Culp Hobby, head of the Department of Health, Education, and Welfare (HEW), stated on this date that "no one could have foreseen the public demand for the Salk vaccine." She was roundly ridiculed in the press for this remark, with many writers and cartoonists taking the trouble to point out that the public had donated millions of dollars to the March of Dimes since 1938 to bring about the Salk vaccine. It was felt that HEW's mismanagement of the Salk vaccine production and allocation process after the successful field trial led to her resignation from HEW on July 13, 1955, just two months after this statement.

July 15, 1955—The Laboratories of Biologics Control was renamed the Bureau of Biologies within the Public Heath System in direct response to the polio vaccine problem. The bureau was greatly expanded, and by 1956 it had over 100 people alone testing vaccines in the polio division.

July 28, 1955— The Mental Health Study Act authorized the surgeon general to award grants to non-government organizations to help support a nationwide study and reevaluation of the problems of mental illness. This act recognized that mental illness was a bigger problem than was previously thought and that newer and more imaginative solutions to the problem were needed.

July 28, 1956— The Alaska Mental Health Enabling Act provided for territorial treatment facilities to eliminate the need to transport mentally ill patients to places outside Alaska (still a territory) for treatment. This act was necessary because Alaska did not become a state until January 3, 1959.

August 2, 1956— The Health Amendments Act of 1956 authorized the surgeon general to assist in increasing the number of adequately trained nurses and professional public health personnel. A shortage of nurses has plagued the public health system for much of its existence.

August 3, 1956— The National Library of Medicine Act placed the Armed Forces Medical Library under the control of the Public Health Service, and renamed it the National Library of Medicine.

November 27, 1957— The Center for Aging Research was established on this date as a focus for National Institutes of Health activities in the field of gerontology. This was another indication of a national shift in health priorities to the diseases of aging.

July 12, 1960— The International Health Research Act was passed on this date. The act authorized the surgeon general to establish and make grants for fellowships in the United States and participating foreign countries. The act included funds for equipment and materials and participation in appropriate international conferences and such. This recognized the reality that much first-class research work in matters related to health was going on in foreign countries, and it would be advantageous for the United States to take an active role in being able to utilize the results of that research.

December 1, 1961— The *California's Health* publication of this date pointed out that as of 1961, the California State Department of Public Health had 8 divisions, 22 bureaus, 7 laboratories, and 5 miscellaneous subdivisions. This reflected not only the fragmentation of public health administration at the time as noted before (*see entry for* July 15, 1953) but also the blurring of the lines between public health and general welfare activities. The renaming in 1979 of the federal Department of Health, Education, and Welfare created in 1953 as the Department of Health and Social Services confirmed this approach. In 1965, New York City Health Commissioner George James declared that the third leading cause of death in New York City was poverty. For the rest of the twentieth century and into the twenty-first, public health in the minds of many officials would encompass what used to be known as welfare activities in addition to or even rather than medically-oriented activities.

March 1962— The trivalent Sabin oral polio vaccine was released and used to immunize millions of children and adults by the end of 1962. In a way this event marked the final victory in the battle against polio in the United States, but it also essentially marked a new era in the development of live-virus vaccines against diseases such as measles, mumps, and rubella.

October 17, 1962— A new act passed this day authorized the surgeon general to establish the National Institute of General Medical Sciences. This new activity would conduct and support research in the basic medical sciences and related behavioral sciences that was relevant to two different institutes or outside the general area of responsibility of any existing institute.

The new act also authorized the creation of the National Institute of Child Health and Human Development. This new institute would conduct and support research and training relating to maternal health, child health, and health programs in human development with special emphasis on the health problems of mothers and children.

October 24, 1963— The Maternal and Child Health and Mental Retardation Planning Amendments of 1963 that were established on this date amended the Social Security Act of 1935 by authorizing a series of grants to prevent mental retardation and increase services for maternal and child health, including crippled children. Funds and grants were also made to the states for similar services. A week later, a companion measure was passed authorizing construction programs for facilities to create mental retardation research centers and community health centers and to train teachers of mentally retarded and other handicapped children.

January 11, 1964— The report of the Surgeon General's Advisory Committee on Smoking and Health was released on this date. Now known as the first *Surgeon General's Report on Smoking and Health*, it was deliberately released on a Saturday morning to avoid an immediate negative reaction by the stock market. The first two copies of the 387-page report were hand-delivered to the West Wing of the White House at 7:30 A.M., and reporters were invited at 9:00 A.M. to a secure auditorium in the State Department, where they were locked in while they read the report and asked questions of Surgeon General Dr. Luther Terry and his advisory committee.

The report concluded that cigarette smoking causes lung cancer and other serious diseases, and thus is "a health hazard of sufficient importance ... to warrant appropriate remedial action." In response, Congress adopted the Federal Cigarette Labeling Act of 1965 and the Public Health Service (PHS) Cigarette Smoking Act of 1969. These laws required a health warning on cigarette packs, banned cigarette advertising in the broadcast media, and called for an annual report on the health consequences of smoking.

This series of reports over the last 40 years has seen a substantial drop in the number of people in the United States who smoke. In the public as a whole, since the initial report was published, the incidence of smoking has fallen from about 42 percent to about 25 percent, with almost half of living adults who ever smoked giving up smoking. Among doctors, who see the deadly effects of smoking up close, the incident of smoking fell from about 79 percent to just over 3 percent. That infers that 96 percent of doctors who once smoked quit.

The report and its aftermath demonstrate how effective the PHS can be in the area of education. The smoking cessation story would be even better if it were not for the number of young adults, especially women, who take up smoking for the first time. The PHS is now targeting educational programs for this group to stop them from adopting the habit (the fact that lung cancer has a higher death rate among women than breast cancer, and has had for almost the last two decades, should help). The results of this report led to a greater emphasis on educational programs by the PHS.

August 27, 1964— An amendment passed on this date focused on public health training by authorizing public health traineeships and training grants to schools of public health, nursing, and engineering.

September 19, 1964— The Public Health Appropriations Act of 1965 passed on this date authorized a $10 million virus-leukemia program. This reflected the thought at the time that at least some cancers were caused by a virus and appropriate research might lead to some sort of protective vaccine. But no such vaccine has been found to date, even though much progress has been made in developing new weapons to deal with cancer, especially including some forms of leukemia.

July 14, 1965— On this date, President Lyndon B. Johnson signed the Older Americans Act. In addition to creating the Administration on Aging, it authorized grants to states for community planning and services programs, as well as research, demonstration, and training projects in the field of aging.

Later amendments to the act would add grants to area agencies on aging for local needs identification, planning, and funding of services, including but not limited to nutrition programs in the community as well as for those who are homebound; programs which served Native American elders, services targeted at low-income minority elders, health promotion and disease prevention activities; in-home services for frail elders; and those services which protect the rights of older persons, such as long-term care ombudsmen.

July 30, 1965 — President Johnson signed a bill establishing the Medicare program. Essentially, the bill meant that all persons 65 years of age and older would be covered by a national health insurance program. The Medicare program would begin on July 1, 1966.

August 31, 1965 — A supplemental appropriations act was passed on this date to address the request of a Presidential Commission on Heart Disease, Cancer, and Stroke. The commission requested that more funds be allocated to the national institutes concerned with these diseases to intensify and support research into these three major killer diseases. This was in a way an acknowledgment that these three killer diseases, with heart disease at the top, had long since replaced all types of infectious diseases (even if all infectious disease death rates were added together) as the prime focus of both public health and medicine in the United States.

November 1, 1966 — A Division of Environmental Health Sciences was established within the National Institutes of Health to conduct, foster, and coordinate research on the biological, chemical, and physical effects of environmental agents.

January 1, 1967 — The National Institute of Mental Health was separated from the National Institutes of Health and raised to bureau status in the Public Health Service (PHS). This step demonstrated the heightened importance of programs concerned with mental health within the PHS.

August 8, 1967 — On this date an employee of the Behring Works in Marburg, Germany, a plant that produced vaccines made from the kidney cells of green monkeys imported from Uganda came down with a viral fever. The man, known only in records by the name of Klaus F., died two weeks later and was the first known victim of what was later called the Marburg virus. Eventually 31 people caught the virus in Marburg. Seven died, a fatality rate approaching 25 percent. This is now known to be a typical death rate for the virus.

The Marburg virus is now identified as a member of the filovirus family. The name is taken from the Latin word for "thread virus." The filovirus looks like a thread rather than the ball shape assumed by most viruses that has been described as being like a peppercorn. Filoviruses have also been described as looking like worms or snakes or strands of rope. Some even wrap themselves into rings. Marburg was the first virus known to assume a ring shape.

The importance of the identification of the filovirus is that the Marburg virus and its much more lethal cousins, the various types of the Ebola virus (*see entry for* September 1976), are notable filoviruses and are the most lethal viruses that have emerged from the African jungles and rain forests since 1967. They kill humans in days rather than the years it takes the AIDS virus to kill, and the deaths they cause are particularly gruesome, with much organ damage and bleeding. They mutate readily (as does the AIDS/HIV virus), and thus vaccines are very difficult to create. This means that in effect there is no cure and no preventive for these viruses except the human immune system, when it is not overwhelmed by the virus.

Humans appear to get the virus only from monkeys, but the true host of the virus must be some other animal that is not harmed by the virus because the monkeys are killed much too easily by the virus to be its host in nature. The viruses are thought to spread only by direct contact with one of its victims (especially via blood), but on the one hand there is some evidence that certain forms of Ebola have spread via water droplets in the air in certain conditions, while on the other hand many people have been in close contact with victims of the filovirus and have not developed any illness themselves. At the moment, as of 2004, these filovirsues are considered potentially the most dangerous viral threat to humans, and great pains are being taken to track outbreaks of illness that they cause anywhere. Efforts are still being made to attempt to locate their home/host in Africa.

December 29, 1970— President Nixon signed the Occupational Safety and Health Act (OSHA). The mission of OSHA is to prevent work-related injuries, illnesses, and deaths. OSHA began operation in 1971, 120 days after the act was approved. In the next three decades occupational deaths would be cut by 62 percent and injuries reduced by 42 percent.

May 22, 1971— Congress passed into law the Supplemental Appropriations Bill, which included $100 million for cancer research. This action was in response to the president's pledge in the State of the Union Address to carry out "an intensive campaign to find a cure for cancer." The National Cancer Institute was to lead the battle that would absorb far more money in the future, as the president signed the National Cancer Act of 1971 on December 23, 1971. However, because cancer is not one disease but many, curing it would be a largely unsuccessful battle, although many advances would be made in the treatment of cancer in the years ahead.

November 18, 1971— The president signed the Comprehensive Health Manpower Training Act of 1971 to provide increased manpower in the health professions. The accompanying Nurse Training Act of 1971 provided training for an increased number of nurses.

May 16, 1972— The National Sickle Cell Anemia Control Act of 1972 became law. This created a national program for the diagnosis and treatment of this disease which typically occurred primarily in Americans of African descent.

October 25, 1972— In order to focus resources on multiple sclerosis (MS), an incurable disease that primarily struck young adults and those somewhat older causing a general paralysis over time that led to death because the muscles controlling breathing finally failed to work properly, a commission was created by the National Advisory Commission on Multiple Sclerosis Act to determine the most productive avenue of researching possible causes and cures for MS.

April 22, 1974— In response to what seemed to be almost an epidemic of sudden infant death syndrome (SIDS), a devastating event in which parents discover apparently healthy infants dead in their cribs, an act was passed authorizing the gathering of data and the review of cases so that causes might be determined and information disseminated on the syndrome.

May 31, 1974— A National Institute on Aging (NIA) was established by the Research on Aging Act of 1974. The NIA was to conduct and support biomedical, social, and behavioral research and training related to the aging process and the various diseases and other needs of the aged. It was another step in directing the focus of national health programs on the growing number of older persons in the United States and recognizing that the major causes of death in total in the country were those that affected primarily older people.

July 23, 1974— The National Cancer Act Amendments of 1974 authorized $2.6 billion to extend and improve the National Cancer Program. The war on cancer was continuing to absorb funds, but there was very little progress in curing cancer. There were certainly many improvements in treatment approaches and much learning about the nature of cancer, but there was nothing approaching a cure, because a cure for cancer is highly unlikely.

January 4, 1975— The National Arthritis Act established a National Commission on Arthritis and Related Musculoskeletal Diseases. As arthritis is primarily a disease of the elderly, this was another attempt to focus public health initiatives on degenerative diseases, which primarily attack older Americans, as opposed to the prior focus in this century on infectious diseases, which primarily attack younger Americans.

April 22, 1976— Amendments to existing laws were enacted addressing programs within the National Heart and Lung Institute. The new amendments also placed emphasis on blood-related research and changed the name of the Institute to the National Heart, Lung, and Blood Institute. Also, the President's Biomedical Research Panel and the National Commission for the Protection of Human Subjects mandated studies of the implications of public disclosure of information contained in various grant applications and contract proposals. Finally, broad-based genetic disease research was authorized including programs for counseling, testing, and information dissemination about genetically transmitted diseases.

July 6, 1976— On this date a man identified only as Yu G. died of a strange disease in southern Sudan, near the edge of the central African rain forest. Mr. Yu G. became the first identified case, or the so-called index case, of what was later named the Ebola-Sudan virus.

Mr. Yu G. did not go to a hospital but died in his family compound. His family buried him in a traditional tribal way in a homemade grave (later visited by public health officials from around the world looking for the home of the Ebola virus). People Mr. Yu G. had been in close contact with began to come down with the disease, and it soon spread to someone who entered a hospital in the town of Maridi. The hospital staff had been using dirty, unsterilized needles to give patients injections, and the disease quickly spread throughout the hospital. Eventually the surviving medical staff abandoned the hospital, and that ultimately stopped the spread of the disease.

The virus killed about 50 percent of the people who contracted it, and they died very quickly (the fatality rate was about twice that of the Marburg virus —*see entry for* August 8, 1967). When everyone finally took great precautions before contacting anybody after the hospital was abandoned, the virus seemed to fade away with no further victims to infect. Eventually a few hundred people died, and the Sudan strain of the virus was identified later after a another major outbreak of a different, more lethal strain of Ebola took place about 500 miles further into the rain forest in a few months (*see entry for* September 1976).

August 2, 1976— The Pennsylvania Department of Health realized on this date that all of the recent reports of a strange illness that had been pouring in during recent weeks were associated with persons who had attended the

58th Annual Convention of the American Legion's Pennsylvania Chapter held at the Bellvue-Stratford Hotel in Philadelphia from July 21 through July 24. Illness of some sort struck 221 persons, of whom 34 died. The total number of sick people included 72 who did not attend the convention but who were in or near the hotel during the same period.

This result triggered one of the largest epidemic investigations in the history of the United States. The illness was traced to a previously unknown strain of bacteria that was named legionella because the disease had already be named by the press as legionnaires' disease. The Centers for Disease Control (CDC) said the disease turns out to be not particularly rare, with 10,000 to 15,000 people being infected annually (some claim up to 100,000). But because special tests are needed to detect the legionella bacteria, and because its symptoms and disease process are much like those of ordinary pneumonia, many people infected with it never learn they had the legionella bacteria. The CDC estimates that no specific cause is found for almost half of the 500,000 adult pneumonia cases that occur each year in the United States.

This situation can be a problem because the legionella bacteria can be easily destroyed at the source, but if no one knows it was the cause of a death from pneumonia, no investigation is carried out and the source remains contaminated. In the case of the Bellevue-Strafford Hotel, the source was in a hot-water plumbing system that readily carried the bacteria throughout the hotel. The problem was, of course, fixed. But that could not save the hotel. No one wanted to stay in such a deadly place, and it was forced to close in 1979. A landmark in Philadelphia since 1904, the hotel tried to reopen under different names, failed again, cut down the number of rooms and tried again, but nothing succeeded. It is now known as a haunted hotel and has its own website of true ghost stories. The legionella bacteria claimed yet another victim in addition to its human casualties.

September 1976— The exact date the first victim was taken ill (and his or her identity) is unknown, but during this month there was a major outbreak of what proved to an Ebola virus along the Ebola and upper Zaire (Congo) rivers in northern Zaire. Although an estimated 55 villages were eventually affected, the central point of the epidemic proved to be the Yambuku Mission Hospital run by Belgian nuns. The nuns laid out five hypodermic needles at the start of each day, and they used them to give injections during the day with no sterilization between shots except for occasionally dipping the needles in warm water to wash off the blood.

A schoolteacher who had received a shot at the hospital for a mild illness broke out with the serious Ebola illness (contracted from the shot with the dirty needle) in a few days. He died at home and was buried in a traditional tribal way where family members removed blood and other things from his body with bare hands. These family members took sick and died soon after. Almost simultaneously there were similar cases in the 55 small villages surrounding the hospital. First those receiving injections died, then their family members. The staff at the hospital took ill treating the sick villagers, and then the Belgian nuns began to get sick in the same way. One of the Belgian nuns was flown to a hospital in Kinshasa, the capital of Zaire. She died there.

Rumors began to flow out of the jungle of some mysterious force destroying whole villages. Officials from Kinshasa flew to Yambuku to investigate. One of the nurses in Kinshasa who had treated the nun from Yambuku and had been covered with her blood became ill. After wandering the city in desperation, she finally returned to her Kinshasa hospital to be treated. By now rumors of the destruction on the Ebola River had reached Europe including the tale of the sick, wandering nun in Kinshasa. The World Health Organization in Geneva went into action, worried that the nun was carrying (and perhaps spreading) an unknown deadly disease from the jungles of Africa. The president of Zaire ordered a quarantine, backed by soldiers with guns, of the hospital in Kinshasa and the area upriver where the whole thing had started.

Samples of the blood of the original nun from Yambuku had been sent out for analysis, and the Centers for Disease Control (CDC) in Atlanta had gotten a sample. They were able to determine that it was a new virus, and they named it the Ebola virus after the river running near the place in which the outbreak had started. In just a few days in mid–October 1976, doctors from the CDC flew to Africa by way of Geneva, and an international team was formed in Kinshasa to try to stop as well as track the virus (the Sudan virus outbreak was also known by then —*see entry for* July 6, 1976). But the international team had no better luck than the others that preceded it. By the time they reached the areas where the outbreaks had started, the virus had burned itself out. And the team was unable to find the source of the virus.

The nun who wandered the city of Kinshasa died in her quarantined hospital, but she was the last victim to die. Searchers found 37 people she had encountered in her wanderings, but none of them became ill, including one who had shared a bottle of pop with the nun. The nun's blood is now frozen in a number of laboratories as Ebola-Mayinga (the nun's name). It is a test sample of Ebola-Zaire, the most deadly of the filoviruses. It kills nine out of ten people who catch it, compared to 50 percent for Ebola-Sudan and 25 percent for the Marburg virus (*see entry for* August 8, 1967). But no one yet knows for sure where the viruses live in Africa, and if the viruses can spread by other means than direct contact with the blood of a person who has the disease. Nurse Mayinga had Ebola-Zaire, but no one who came in casual contact with her caught the disease. Public health officials everywhere stay on alert, because a virus such as Ebola-Zaire could eliminate the human race if it were easily spread.

October 1976— Following much debate, Congress appropriated $135 million to develop a vaccine for the so-called swine flu virus and initiated the program in this month. The virus developed early in 1976 in other countries, and public health officials in the government feared that it might be a repeat of the epidemic on 1918–19. President Gerald Ford then called for a massive vaccination program, but there was considerable controversy over whether the virus was as dangerous as suggested and how vaccine makers could be protected from anti-trust and other liabilities if they got together to produce enough vaccine in the relatively small time allotted (it was confirmation of the claims of many that Jonas Salk's famous field trial of his polio vaccine in 1954 could never be done in today's litigation-prevalent atmosphere). There were also claims that the whole business was an election year gimmick by Ford.

Finally, about 40 million people were vaccinated by February 1977 before the program was sharply curtailed as the threatened epidemic showed no signs of developing. The event did show that mass vaccination programs could be developed quickly if needed, and some legislative and administrative steps were put in place that could be used in a future emergency.

August 1, 1977— The following public health programs were extended for another year by a law passed on this date: the Medical Library Assistance Program; cancer research and control program; heart, blood vessel, lung, and blood disease research, prevention and control programs; population research and voluntary family planning programs; and sudden infant death syndrome information and counseling programs.

October 22, 1977— The world became free of smallpox with the last known case of naturally acquired smallpox being reported in Somalia, although it wasn't until May 8, 1980, that the World Health Organization officially declared that smallpox had been eliminated everywhere. The last case in the United States had been reported in 1949, and the United States stopped routinely vaccinating for smallpox in 1972. At present the smallpox virus exists only in a frozen state in several countries, but none are willing to destroy their supply in case smallpox is threatened to be used as a weapon, and they would be unable to produce a suitable vaccine. Thus, the frozen smallpox will be held indefinitely in the hope a cure might be developed someday that would erase the threat of smallpox being used as a weapon.

November 9, 1977— The Federal Mine Safety and Health Amendments of 1977 gave the Health, Education, and Welfare Department authority to appoint an advisory committee on coal or other mine-related health research. Coal mining was once one of the most dangerous occupations in the United States, but great strides had been made in safety since the 1930s, and coal mining, although greatly reduced by the use of other fuels, was now one of the safest mining occupations.

November 9, 1978—The secretary of Health, Education, and Welfare was authorized to (1) conduct studies and tests of substances for carcinogenicity, teratogenicity, mutagenicity, and other harmful biological effects, (2) establish and conduct a comprehensive research program on the biological effects of low-level radiation, (3) conduct and support research and studies on human nutrition and (4) publish an annual report which lists all substances known to be carcinogenic and to which a significant number of Americans are exposed.

These actions reflected the increasing amount of litigation beginning to take place concerning the effects on humans of exposure to certain substances considered to be toxic.

January 16, 1980—A Frenchman employed by a sugar factory in western Keyna who had been flown to a hospital in Nairobi suffering from a strange illness died early in the morning on this date in the intensive care unit of the Nairobi hospital. The doctor who attended the man soon came down with apparently the same illness after being vomited on by the sick man. Unable to diagnose or treat the doctor's illness, the hospital sent some of his blood to a virology laboratory in South Africa and also to the Centers for Disease Control in the United States.

The diagnosis came back that the doctor's blood contained a strain of the Marburg virus. This caused great excitement because health officials had been trying to find the origin of the Marburg virus since it appeared in Germany in 1967 (*see entry for* August 8, 1967), but public health bands of searchers sent out at that time to Uganda (from where the monkeys causing the virus in Marburg had been shipped in 1967) were unable to find the virus. Future searchers of the area near the sugar plantation had no better luck.

The Nairobi hospital was temporarily shut down while 67 people who had in some way attended the sick Frenchman and the doctor in the Nairobi hospital who had become sick were quarantined for two weeks. But no one else became ill, and even the doctor who had been vomited on by the Frenchman recovered. The doctor's name was Musoke, and the strain of the Marburg virus he encountered is named the Musoke strain. Samples of his blood remain frozen in various laboratories around the world, including some in the United States. This permits future outbreaks of strange diseases to be compared to the Musoke strain for possible identification.

May 14, 1980— The Department of Health, Education, and Welfare (HEW) was reorganized because a new and separate Department of Education was established. This was the result of an act that was initiated on October 17, 1979. The remaining functions of HEW, including the Public Health Service, were assembled into a new department called the Department of Health and Human Services. This continued the blurring of the line between health in terms of primarily its medical aspects and social services in terms of welfare that had been going on since the end of World War II. To many officials, poverty was seen as a prime cause of disease and death, and thus needed the kind of government attention that would be given to a serious infectious disease, for example.

July 16, 1982— The Centers for Disease Control within the Public Health System (PHS) reported signs of a growing AIDS (acquired immune deficiency syndrome) epidemic. AIDS had produced 184 deaths in the United States since it was first reported in June 1981. In 1984, both PHS and French scientists would identify the HIV virus (human immunodeficiency virus) that causes AIDS, and in 1985 a blood test to detect AIDS would be licensed.

HIV was believed to have originated in Africa sometime between the late 1940s and early 1950s. It is believed to have mutated from the simian immunodeficiency virus (SIV), which causes the same kind of disease in monkeys as does AIDS in humans. It is presumed that humans developed AIDS by eating the raw meat and drinking the blood of infected monkeys. AIDS is spread by sexual contact or by other exchanges of bodily fluids that can enter the victim's blood such as use of an infected needle when injecting drugs.

Many of the early cases of AIDS in the United States were linked to a promiscuous flight attendant who flew around the world (including Africa) spreading AIDS as he went. AIDS is actually a hard disease to get because it requires such intimate contacts or the use of illegal drug injections. In the United States, AIDS never peaked beyond causing about 2 percent of all deaths, which made it about only the tenth leading cause of death. It has fallen well below those numbers today.

AIDS attacks the immune system and often causes death via a disease like pneumonia or kinds of cancer the immune system would otherwise destroy. If one practices safe sex and does not illegally inject drugs, it is very hard to catch AIDS. This limits the disease to narrow segments of the population in the United States, and prescription drugs have been developed to greatly extend the lives of those who have the disease. Thus, it is not statistically a major health problem in the United States. Because it is caused by a virus, there is no antibiotic cure for AIDS, and attempts to develop a vaccine are hindered by the ability of the AIDS virus to mutate (as is the case with a more innocent disease like the flu). In the United States, education is the main weapon against AIDS.

In countries like Africa, where superstition and ignorance abound in conjunction with corrupt political systems, AIDS is a major killer. It can be found in all members of a family and threatens to wipe out whole generations of the population in some areas. But this could be true of many other diseases to come as mankind encroaches more and more on the rain forests and jungles of the world. New diseases are a common occurrence, and where they are met primarily by ignorance and superstition and corrupt governments, these new diseases are very likely to become great killers.

November 16, 1982— Dr. C. Everett Koop, later to become controversial for his outspoken views, was named surgeon general of the Public Health Service.

January 4, 1983—The Orphan Drug Act made changes in the law to encourage development and marketing of orphan drugs. Orphan drugs are drugs for rare diseases or conditions that are not economically feasible for private industry to develop and market. These drugs especially include drugs for rare kinds of cancers and sickle cell disease. This act would be amended in August 1985 to be sure that the intentions of the original act were met and that money was allocated as intended for rare diseases.

July 30, 1983— The supplemental appropriation for the Public Health Service provided funds for the first time for issues related specifically to AIDS (*see entry for* July 16, 1982). About $9.4 million of the appropriation was earmarked for the National Institutes of Health, and another $5.9 million was earmarked for the National Laboratories for Microbiology and the development of a Biomedical Information Communication Center in Portland, Oregon.

October 19, 1984— The National Organ Transplant Act authorized the secretary general to establish a task force on organ procurement and transportation, to examine relevant issues, and report to the Congress within 12 months. Transplantation had by now become so commonplace that it was felt to be necessary to define policies and procedures covering the process. After the beginning of the twenty-first century, there would be approximately 25,000 transplants performed each year and over 80,000 patients waiting for a transplant. Some patients were waiting for more than one organ transplant, but there were three times as many people waiting for transplants as there were operations performed. The major holdup, of course, was the lack of available organs. But transplantations had become so successful that many doctors now recommended it where previously the patient ultimately would have simply shown up as a death statistic. As often happens in the field of medicine, it took less than 50 years for transplantation to move from a miracle of science to a relatively routine operation.

November 14, 1986—For the first time, an act was established considering Alzheimer's disease. The Alzheimer's Disease and Related Dementias Services Research Act established an interagency council and advisory panel on Alzheimer's disease (AD). It authorized the director of the National Institutes of Health to make awards for distinguished research on AD, to plan for and conduct research, to establish an AD clearinghouse, to make a grant or enter into a contract with a national organization representing Alzheimer's patients, to establish an information system and national toll-free telephone line, and to provide information as well as safety and transportation personnel to caregivers of Alzheimer's patients.

Alzheimer's disease had been growing substantially in the United States as the population aged, and finally required an act to address it specifically. By 1999, Alzheimer's disease made the list of the ten leading causes of death for the first time, and it would continue its way up the list as the twenty-first century continued.

July 23, 1987—President Reagan named a 13–member commission on the HIV epidemic, and the commission held its first meeting immediately after the announcement.

September 1, 1987—The National Institutes of Health (NIH) became a smoke-free agency, banning smoking in all buildings. This would become a common practice across the United States eventually, and it demonstrates how successful the anti-smoking educational program was that started in earnest after the publication of the surgeon general's report on smoking in 1964 and grew in the years that followed.

October 8, 1987—A public law was passed on this date designating October 1, 1987, as National Medical Research Day. This acknowledged 100 years of contributions by the National Institutes of Health and other federally supported research institutions to improving the health and well being of "Americans and all humankind."

November 29, 1987—An amendment to the Older Americans Act (*see entry for* July 14, 1965) addressed Alzheimer's disease research and authorized the director of the National Institute on Aging (NIA) to provide for conducting clinical trials on therapeutic agents recommended for further analysis by NIA and the Federal Drug Administration. It also authorized the president to call a White House Conference on Aging in 1991.

December 22, 1987— The new appropriation amount approved on this date for the National Institutes of Health included $448 million for AIDS. This amount was to be allocated among the various institutes for their various research efforts for AIDS.

October 4, 1988— The secretary of Health and Human Services was authorized to make grants to the states to provide drugs that were determined to be able to prolong the life of individuals suffering from AIDS.

November 4, 1988— A new bill extended a moratorium on fetal research for two more years through November 4, 1990. This issue would remain controversial through the rest of the 1990s and into the new century through today.

Another part of the bill established the foundation for a federal policy on AIDS. In addition to ongoing research, provisions were made for information dissemination, education, prevention, anonymous testing, and establishment of a National Commission on AIDS. The review process for AIDS-related grants was expedited, provision was made for priority requests for personnel and administrative support, a clinical research review committee was established, the AIDS outpatient capacity at the clinical center was doubled, community-based clinical trails were mandated, awards for international clinical research were authorized, and information services were expanded. An Office of AIDS research was established, and even a program was authorized to repay loans for scientists who agreed to conduct AIDS research while employed at the National Institutes of Health.

It was an extensive program that would eventually control the AIDS epidemic in the United States. AIDS continued to be a deadly disease, but the rate of new cases eventually declined (in 2000, new cases were only 57 percent of the amount in 1995), persons with AIDS lived longer (the number of deaths due to AIDS in 2000 was one-third of the total in 1995), and only a relatively narrow portion of the public was impacted. AIDS would never reach the status of a national emergency as it would in other countries, especially in Africa.

May 22, 1989— The National Institutes of Health conducted its first gene transfer in humans on this date. A cancer patient was infused with lymphocytes that had been altered by inserting a gene.

November 29, 1989— In an often little-noticed part of medical research, an act was passed to provide for the construction of biomedical facilities in order to ensure a continued supply of specialized strains of mice essential to biomedical research in the United States.

December 7, 1989— On this date a special army team destroyed the last of almost 500 monkeys kept in a building near Reston, Virginia. The monkeys were sent from here to be used in various medical facilities for biological experiments. The monkeys had been sent from the Philippines (but could have interacted with monkeys from other countries during shipping) and had come down with what proved to be a strain of the Ebola filovirus (*see entry for* September 1976). The monkeys were being rapidly killed by the virus, but the prime concern was that a virus as deadly as Ebola had suddenly appeared in the United States. Some workers at the facility had taken ill, and there was great apprehension that they might spread the virus. The Centers for Disease Control had been called in to handle this part of the problem.

As it turned out, none of the sick or exposed workers died. All recovered rather easily, although four developed antibodies to the virus. The virus was named Ebola-Reston, and it appears to have the odd quality that it destroys monkeys very easily but does not seriously affect humans. However, other strains of Ebola, such as Ebola-Zaire, kill up to 90 percent of their human victims.

There have been other outbreaks of Ebola since those described in this book, and researchers still do not know where the virus originates in Africa nor what animal is its host. It is not clear if the virus can spread in any other way than direct contact with the blood of a victim. It is probable that other outbreaks will occur in the future wherever humans and large monkey populations come in contact. Public health officials in the United States and other countries keep a constant outlook for outbreaks.

August 18, 1990— The Ryan White Comprehensive AIDS Resources Emergency (CARE) Act of 1990 was passed on this date. The act authorized the National Institutes of Health to make demonstration grants to community health centers and other entities providing primary health care and servicing a significant number of pediatric patients and pregnant women with HIV disease.

Ryan White was a 18-year-old boy from Indiana who died of AIDS on April 8, 1990. He had the rare disease of hemophilia, and he had to have regular blood transfusions as part of the treatment for the disease. Because blood products were not yet fully screened in the 1980s for the HIV virus that causes AIDS, Ryan White contracted AIDS from his transfusions. As he was a white, middle-class heterosexual who did not take illegal drugs, he did not fit the normal profile of people who contracted AIDS (primarily homosexual men and people who took illegal drugs intravenously). After he developed AIDS, he was expelled from school as a health risk. This led to his becoming a symbol for AIDS education.

There was an understandable furor when White was expelled, and as the AIDS epidemic was just getting underway in terms of deaths and the number of new cases, White was used as an example that literally anyone could get AIDS. However, since AIDS could not be spread by casual contact, the victims of the disease could interact normally in society with a few precautions. White was admitted to another school where everyone had been educated about the nature of AIDS and HIV.

Before his death, White worked on educating people about AIDS. After his death, the act bearing his name was passed in Congress only four months later. The act was amended and re-authorized in May 1996 with four more years of funding.

November 5, 1990— A new act called on the Public Health Service (PHS) to review periodically the recommended frequency for performing screening mammography. There has been an ongoing controversy in this area with some complaining that the uncomfortable test is performed too frequently. But data continues to show that the procedure saves lives, and many physicians feel it is a relatively small price to pay for its life-savings benefits. If the PHS establishes a standard, most doctors will follow it regardless of their personal opinions.

November 15, 1990— Reflecting increasing national concerns about the health effects of air pollution, a new act directed the Public Health Service to perform research on human health risks relevant to air pollution, with special notice being given to the effects of mercury in the air.

November 16, 1990— The broad scope of the Public Health Service (PHS) was demonstrated by an act directing the PHS to provide grants for the training and education of workers who are or may be engaged in activities related to hazardous waste removal, containment or emergency response. The legislation was entitled the Hazardous Materials Transportation Uniform Safety Act of 1990.

November 7, 1991— National Basketball Association (NBA) All-Star Earvin (Magic) Johnson of the Los Angeles Lakers announced at a news conference today that he contacted the virus HIV that causes AIDS and was retiring from professional basketball at the age of 32. Johnson's announcement caused a notorious sensation at the time, but it turned out to be an important part of the AIDS education process in the United States and throughout the world.

Many people at the time did not understand the distinction between being infected with the virus HIV and having a full-blown case of AIDS.

Johnson very publicly began taking an "AIDS cocktail," a mixture of drugs that was intended to delay the onset of AIDS. At the time, it typically took 8 to 12 years to progress from being HIV positive to dying from AIDS. But many improvements had been made in AIDS drugs, and Johnson showed no signs of having even developed the start of AIDS 13 years after his announcement. The new drug developments have also extended the life spans of people with an active case of AIDS, and Johnson, at the age of 45, can look forward to approaching the normal lifespan (67) for his year of birth (1959).

Johnson further contributed to AIDS education by returning to play basketball both professionally and in the 1992 Olympics. Although there was some controversy at the time — it is very easy to be scratched and draw blood in basketball — it was shown that with some simple precautions an HIV-positive individual could still safety play basketball. Johnson became a successful businessman, including leading a group of players in very profitable basketball game exhibitions around the world. He wrote a book in 1992 titled *What You Can Do to Avoid AIDS*, and as a non-homosexual non-drug-using black man who had contacted AIDS from unsafe heterosexual sex, he emphasized the need to practice safe sex and was an important role model for many people at the time.

October 24, 1992 — The Public Health Service (PHS) was directed by the Cancer Registries Act to establish a national program of cancer registries with a prime goal of assuring minimal standards for quality and completeness of cancer case information. The act also directed the PHS to conduct a study to determine why the breast cancer mortality rates in nine states and the District of Columbia were elevated compared to the rest of the states.

November 4, 1992 — The Public Health Service was directed to work with the National Aeronautical and Space Administration to coordinate biomedical research activities relative to areas where microgravity environments may contribute to significant progress in the understanding and treatment of diseases and other medical conditions. The two agencies were specifically to work with the republics of the former Soviet Union in this area, reflecting the ongoing activities with the former Soviet Union and its space station.

December 14, 1993 — The Public Health Service was directed to pursue research into the cause, early detection of, and prevention and treatment of tuberculosis. This is an example of a disease that was considered conquered in the United States, but one that has arisen again as a problem because immigrant populations, many arriving here illegally, bring tuberculosis with them from their homelands. In many parts of the world, many old diseases by the standards of the United States, like tuberculosis, never went away internationally when they essentially vanished in the United States. Thus, they reappear again in a reminder that any disease anywhere is a potential problem to our public health in our interconnected world.

October 25, 1994— The Public Health Service was directed to establish an Office of Dietary Supplements to conduct and coordinate research relating to dietary supplements and determine the extent to which their use reduces the risk of certain diseases.

November 5, 1994— On this date, President Ronald Reagan, who served as president from 1980 through 1988, announced he had recently been diagnosed with the beginnings of Alzheimer's disease. This disease, which now affects an estimated 4.5 million Americans, is an incurable degenerative disease of the brain that over time turns its victims into a state of essentially total helplessness, as if they were once more a small child. Cogitative abilities are lost, and victims often fail to recognize long-time family members and friends.

President Reagan said he was announcing his condition publicly because in the past when he and his wife each suffered from cancer, public announcements were made that triggered many people to have appropriate screening tests that led to diagnosis of cancer when it was still curable. Although there is no cure for Alzheimer's, early intervention can often be helpful, and raising awareness of a disease can often help to increase the effort to find a cure.

President Reagan was almost 84 years old when he made his announcement. Alzheimer's is estimated to exist in 10 percent of the population over 65, and almost half of the population over 85. The rate of progression of Alzheimer's varies from 3 to 20 years, but on average the period of time from the onset of symptoms to death is about eight years. President Reagan died on June 5, 2004, nine and-a-half years after his announcement.

March 1, 1995— The Social Security Administration became an independent agency within the federal government, separating from the Health and Human Services Department in order to permit each agency to focus more directly on its specific and ever-growing task.

January 26, 1996— The Public Health Service was prohibited from using any funds for human embryo research for at least the duration of the 1996 fiscal year.

April 24, 1996— As part of a broad Antiterrorism Act, the Public Health Service (PHS) was directed to establish safety procedures for the use of biological agents, training in handling and proper laboratory containment, safeguards to prevent their use for criminal purposes, and procedures to protect the public safety. However, the PHS must ensure availability of biological agents for research purposes.

July 29, 1996— The Public Health Service (PHS), in accordance with the Traumatic Brain Injury Act, was to provide for the conduct of expanded studies and the establishment of innovative programs with respect to traumatic brain injury. The focus was to award contracts and grants to outside interests rather than increase such programs within the PHS.

August 6, 1996— A reauthorization of the Clean Water Act directed the Public Health Service to cooperate with the Environmental Protection Agency to work within the tougher standards of the act and announce an interim national drinking water regulation in the case of a contaminant due to an urgent threat to public health.

September 30, 1996— The prohibition against using Public Health Service funds for research on human embryos was continued. The prohibition was again continued in October 1998.

August 5, 1997— An increase of $150 million was authorized in the funds allocated for research within the Public Health Service into the prevention and care of Type 1 diabetes.

October 21, 1998— An extensive act passed today include prohibitions on the use of Public Health Service (PHS) funds for programs for sterile needle distribution and for promoting the legalization of controlled substances except in certain very specific limited circumstances. However, language in the act directed the PHS to consult with other groups to establish criteria for evaluation of substance abuse treatment and prevention programs.

The same act included directives on research for prostrate cancer, juvenile diabetes, Alzheimer's disease, Parkinson's disease, and multiple sclerosis.

October 31, 1998— Various amendments relative to women's health research directed the Public Health Service to continue research concerning the drug DES (diethylstilbestrol); osteoporosis, Paget's disease and related disorders; breast, ovarian, and related cancers; heart attack, stroke, and other cardiovascular diseases; and aging processes.

November 29, 1999— An new appropriations act for fiscal year 2000 provided the National Institutes of Health within the Public Health Service a $2.3 billion increase in funding over fiscal year 1999. Included in the funding was the Newborn and Infant Screening and Intervention Act, which directed the National Institute of Deafness and Other Communication Disorders to carry out a program of research on the efficacy of new screening techniques and technology, including clinical trials of screening methods, studies on the efficacy of intervention, and related basic and applied research on hearing loss in newborns.

July 10, 2000— A Radiation Exposure and Compensation Act authorized the Public Health Service to establish a grant program to states for education, prevention, and early detection of radiogenic cancers and diseases.

July 28, 2000— The U.S. Postal Service was authorized to issue semipostal stamps to support breast cancer research within the National Institutes of Health (NIH) of the Public Health Service. The profits from this stamp are split. The NIH receives 70 percent and the Department of Defense receives 30 percent for its breast cancer research program.

October 17, 2000— The Children's Health Act of 2000 authorized federal programs for research and other activities related to autism, fragile X, juvenile arthritis, juvenile diabetes, asthma, hearing loss, epilepsy, traumatic brain injuries, childhood skeletal malignancies, muscular dystrophy, autoimmune diseases, and birth defects and genetic mental impairment among other conditions. This sobering list demonstrates the possible problems of childhood even without the presence of previous deadly infectious diseases.

November 6, 2000— An act with the unusual name of the Needlestick Prevention and Safety Act required changes in the blood-borne pathogen standards in effect under the Occupational Safety and Health Act of 1970 to protect workers whose occupations expose them to pathogens such as HIV. Employers are required to use needles and associated devices with built-in safety mechanisms to reduce accidental punctures. They must also keep a log of such needlestick injuries in a way that protects the confidentiality of injured employees.

November 13, 2000— A compilation of bills included a directive that the National Institute of Arthritis and Musculoskeletal and Skin Diseases expand and intensify research and related activities regarding the disease of lupus. Further, the Alzheimer's Disease Clinical Research and Training program was created within the National Institute on Aging.

December 20, 2000— In an act that demonstrates the incredible detail the Public Health Service must deal with in discharging its responsibilities, the Chimpanzee Health Improvement, Maintenance, and Protections Act required the National Institutes of Health (NIH) to contract with a nonprofit entity to create a sanctuary system for the long-term care of chimpanzees that are no longer needed in research conducted or supported by NIH, the Food and Drug Administration, and other federal agencies. Chimpanzees that have entered into the system cannot be used again for research except in very specific circumstances.

May 24, 2001— The Public Health Service is directed to work with the Department of Agriculture on a report to Congress concerning research programs, diagnostic tools and preventive and therapeutic agents, and monitoring programs regarding foot-and-mouth disease, bovine spongiform encephalopathy, variant Creutzfield-Jacobs disease, and related diseases in the United States. The line between important animal diseases that can affect the food supply and conventional public health actions is a thin one when it comes to applying national resources to national problems.

September 11, 2001— Attacks by terrorists destroyed the Twin Towers of the World Trade Center in New York and raised concerns about related attacks in the form of bioterrorism. The Public Health Service (PHS) quickly begins to address this area, and as described in the listing for January 10, 2002, the Department of Defense requested the PHS to carry out some specific actions.

January 4, 2002— An act is reauthorized to improve the safety and efficacy of pharmaceuticals for children. Studies for the use of drugs in the pediatric population for purposes other than which they were originally labeled are especially encouraged. Other related studies are suggested for federal entities that have the expertise to conduct pediatric clinical trials (such as the Public Health Service).

January 10, 2002— In response to the terrorist attacks of September 11, 2001, the Department of Defense provided funding for the Public Health Service (PHS) through the National Institutes of Health (NIH) to perform a number of actions. They included having the National Institute of Allergy and Infectious Diseases conduct research on safer alternatives to the existing smallpox vaccine, such as an inactivated smallpox virus. Because there still is no cure for smallpox, fears have always existed that terrorists would try to make use of existing stocks of the virus, and vaccinating the entire country in a timely manner would be very difficult.

Also, the PHS is provided with funds to construct a level-4 biosafety laboratory, and to improve laboratory security at the Centers for Disease

Control and the NIH. Finally, funds are included for the National Institute of Environmental Health Sciences to carry out worker training, research, and education activities in response to the terrorist attack.

May 14, 2002— The National Cancer Institute within the Public Health Service (PHS) is directed to expand and coordinate blood cancer research programs, particularly with respect to leukemia, lymphoma, and multiple myeloma. The PHS is also asked to establish a related education program for patients and the general public.

June 12, 2002— The Public Health Security and Bioterrorism Preparedness and Response Act of 2002 amended the Public Heath Service Act to strengthen protection related to public health. The Public Health Service is directed to establish a joint interdepartmental working group with other federal agencies on preparedness for acts of bioterrorism. This working group is to provide consultations on, assistance in, and recommendations regarding provision of appropriate safety and health training; coordination and prioritization of countermeasures to treat, prevent, or identify exposures to biological agents; and research on pathogens likely to be used in a biological threat or attack on the civilian population.

July 11, 2002— In a report published today in the online version of *Science*, researchers claimed to have created a synthetic version of the poliovirus. It was less potent than the real thing because of changes introduced into the genome sequence to identify it as a synthetic virus, but it nevertheless paralyzed and killed the laboratory animals it was tested on when the dose was high enough. The creators at the Stony Brook campus of the University of New York said the motive for their work was to prove it could be done and thus alert the world to the fact that properly skilled terrorists could do it. Thus, it could be another threat public health systems would have to be prepared to deal with.

The synthetic poliovirus that was created is considerably simpler to create than the virus that produces smallpox, for example, but if viruses can be created by just using the published genome code, the fact creates a new threat to world health, even if the technique was not used by terrorists. There is no known way at present to combat diseases produced by viruses except by using vaccines to prevent the disease from causing new infections. But if the virus mutates (as many do, including flu and AIDS), a vaccine may not be possible. The problems of protecting the public from disease continually grow more complicated.

October 26, 2002— The Public Health Service was directed to authorize the National Institutes of Health (NIH) to conduct or support research to examine the long-term health implications of gel- and saline-filled breast implants. This includes studies to develop and examine techniques to measure concentrations of silicone in body fluids and tissues and to track silicone breast implant recipients. The NIH is to submit a report to Congress within six months describing the status of the research.

November 2, 2002 — The Public Health Service (PHS) is directed through the National Institute of Drug Addiction to expand ongoing research and clinical trials relative to drug abuse and addiction. The PHS is to report on the results from the standpoint of biomedical, behavioral, and social issues. A specific study of methamphetamine treatment is also requested.

November 6, 2002 — The Public Health Service, through the National Institutes of Health (NIH) and its Office of Rare Diseases, is directed to recommend an agenda for research on rare diseases, promote coordination and cooperation among NIH Institutes and Centers, promote sufficient allocation of NIH resources related to rare diseases, promote the establishment of a centralized rare disease information clearing house, and prepare a biennial report on rare disease activities.

November 25, 2002 — The Homeland Security Act of 2002 established a new executive branch agency known as the United States Department of Homeland Security (DHS). Within the DHS is a Directorate of Science and Technology that is to develop projects for DHS as required, but excluding those related to human health–related research and development activities. The Secretary of Health and Human Services (HHS), which includes the Public Health Service (PHS), is directed to set priorities, goals, objectives, and policies and to develop a coordinated strategy for the appropriate activities of the DHS and the PHS.

December 18, 2002 — The Public Health Service is directed to renew funding for its special diabetes programs for Type 1 diabetes research and also a parallel services program for diabetes in Native Americans.

February 14, 2003 — Dolly, the cloned sheep, was euthanized on this date due to an incurable lung infection. Dolly had been the first mammal to be cloned from an adult cell, and was born amid much fanfare on July 5, 1996. A year earlier, Dolly had been reported to have developed premature arthritis. She was about six-and-a-half years old on this date (sheep can live to be 11 to 12 years old), and doctors could not determine if her deadly lung infection or her arthritis had anything to do with her cloned status. Dolly's birth had intensified the worldwide debate about cloning, a debate which still goes on amid various reports of different cloning feats. Some reports even claim to have cloned a human being, but none of these reports have yet proven valid.

February 27, 2003—A new kind of pneumonia known as severe acute respiratory syndrome (SARS), which appeared to originate in Asia, was first documented on this date. There were fears of a pandemic, but the disease was apparently contained by July 2003.

April 14, 2003—The completion of the Human Genome Project was announced on this date. The project, which was meant to determine or sequence the order of the four chemical bases that make up DNA and carry the genetic code for the human race, took 13 years (two fewer than originally projected) and cost $2.7 billion. A draft sequence had been published three years earlier, but today's data was more accurate and more comprehensive. It had been arranged to publish it on this date to commemorate the 50th anniversary of the determination of the structure of DNA by James Watson and Francis Crick in April 1953.

The practical use of the genome was hoped to be the ongoing discovery of genetic remedies to many serious diseases. These discoveries would indicate the directions public health initiatives should take in the future.

June 27, 2003—The Medicare Prescription Drug, Improvement, and Modernization Act was passed today by Congress. This act created a voluntary, federally subsidized outpatient prescription drug benefit with additional subsidies for certain low-income Medicare beneficiaries. Other improvements were made in the Medicare program, and a new agency was created within the Department of Health and Human Services to administer the program. The drug benefit would not begin until 2006, but additional acts were planned before 2004 that would offer some initial benefits between 2004 and 2006.

December 8, 2003—The Medicare Prescription Drug Discount Card and Transitional Assistance Program was enacted into law on this date. This was part of the Medicare Prescription Drug, Improvement, and Modernization Act of 2003 (*see entry for* June 27, 2003). Recognizing that in today's world prescription drugs are a much bigger part of medical costs than they were when Medicare began in 1965, Congress agreed to begin a Medicare drug program beginning on January 1, 2006. The discount card program was an attempt to provide some immediate relief to seniors and disabled persons before the overall drug program begins in 2006.

Starting in May 2004, the law passed today would permit certain Medicare beneficiaries to enroll in a discount drug card program. Beginning in June 2004, the discounts would actually take effect. In addition, Medicare will provide $600 in cash assistance in 2004 and another $600 in 2005 for low-income Medicare beneficiaries. This new program is not considered an actual prescription drug program but rather a stopgap measure to help certain groups until the new Medicare drug program officially gets underway in 2006.

January 11, 2004— This date marked the 40th anniversary of the first *Surgeon General's Report on Smoking and Health* (*see entry for* January 11, 1964). Some analysts have pointed out that it is not only the reduction in smoking in the United States that can be credited to this report and its successors but the conversion of the attitude about smoking over the last 40 years. Once it was considered cool to be a smoker, but now we accept — even expect — that there is no smoking in workplaces, public buildings, bars, restaurants, airplanes, buses, courtrooms, and even some outdoor stadiums and beaches. The proven dangers of second-hand smoke have made it no longer a private choice whether to smoke where other people are gathered. This situation was unthinkable in 1964, but now it is the norm. The United States is much more protective of its citizens in this respect than many other countries, but it clearly is no longer cool to smoke (and scatter cigarette butts) in the United States.

April 4, 2004— A trend towards smaller serving sizes at fast-food stores, restaurants, and products available in grocery stores was noted by an article in the *Los Angeles Times* dated today. The sizes of such things as soft drinks, cheeseburgers, and candy bars have been growing for the last three decades, and now smaller sizes are starting to become available in a trend that suppliers say is a response to a perceived demand by customers.

This is part of the desperate attempt by most Americans to lose weight, but it is not clear if smaller serving sizes will result in the consumption of less food overall. Eating more units of a smaller item will not result in lost weight, and eating more snacks to make up for the smaller size servings consumed in a regular meals will not help either. But having more choices available may help some people eat less in total.

May 28, 2004— New reports recently released by the surgeon general and the Center for Disease Control and Prevention showed that smoking was even more dangerous to health than previously thought. An article in the *Los Angeles Times* of this date quoted officials as saying that smoking adversely affects nearly every organ in the body. Essentially, tobacco smoke and its by-products travel everywhere in the body that the blood travels, causing unhealthy effects of some sort. In addition, data shows that babies exposed to second-hand smoke are twice as likely to die from sudden infant death syndrome (SIDS) as those not so exposed, and babies whose mother smokes before and after birth are three to four times at greater risk.

June 7, 2004— The issue of *Time* carrying this date had a special section on obesity. It noted that two-thirds of American adults are officially over-weight, and about half of those are officially "obese," a category considered dangerous to health. About 15 percent of children less than age 19 are also overweight. The appendix in this book shows that when causes of death in the United States are listed by cause instead of by disease, the leading killer is tobacco, which causes 18 percent of all deaths. However, the second lead-ing cause is poor diet and physical activity, which is close behind at almost 17 percent. The third leading cause, alcohol, is far behind at 3.5 percent, and all other causes are even further behind.

This means that obesity is not just a question of esthetics, it is a ques-tion of an increased risk of premature death. Probably the topic of how to lose weight is the subject of more books and diet plans than any other sin-gle subject. People recognize the need to lose weight, but they seem unable to do it. A recent poll taken in connection with the article showed that 58 percent of Americans would like to lose weight. There is a certain irony in the fact that in many parts of the world the prime worry is starvation, while in other parts the concern is eating too much. But no one at either end of this scale enjoys the irony. The hard fact is that about 38 percent of the deaths in the United States are due to basic lifestyle choices — whether to smoke, overeat and not get an appropriate amount of exercise, or consume alcohol in excess. The best action public health officials can take against this prob-lem is to continually educate people about the implications of their lifestyle choices.

June 7, 2004— An article in the *Los Angeles Times* of this date noted that many physicians were recommending that children in their early years and even infants, if they were born prematurely, should be screened for high blood pressure. The disease has many bad effects and catching it early would help in starting treatment before some of those bad effects become manifest.

June 22, 2004— In testimony before Congress on this date, the National Institutes of Health (NIH) said it would dramatically tighten policies that address consulting deals between drug companies and scientists at NIH. According to a subsequent story in the *Los Angeles Times* the director of the NIH, Elias A. Zerhouni, said that perhaps he should have acted sooner to crack down on deals where scientists receive payments from the drug companies that may create a conflict of interest.

With the NIH so intimately involved in anything that affects public health (the NIH will spend about $28 billion on medical research this year), the drug companies are naturally anxious to maintain good relationships with NIH scientists in many ways, including the offering of lucrative consulting contracts with key scientists. There is nothing basically illegal in doing so, but certain guidelines have to be established and followed to be sure objectivity in performing and awarding contracts is maintained. Where so much money is involved, and thousands of people are also involved, there is always the danger that certain individuals will abuse the system. This is the problem that the NIH said it would focus on more strongly in the future.

June 23, 2004 — A story in the *Los Angeles Times* today told how a polio outbreak in Nigeria was crippling young children and threatened an epidemic in a large part of Africa. The problem was due to the usual combination of fear, ignorance, and political corruption. Muslim religious leaders in one area had told their followers to avoid the polio vaccine because it was a plot to affect the fertility of Muslim women and thus reduce the Muslim population. No matter how good the technology the World Health Organization brings to different regions of the world, it is no match for ignorance and the lies of so-called leaders. In the United States such problems can be encountered on an individual basis but rarely at a level that large groups of people are affected. The story shows that intelligent public health actions in one area can be undone by unintelligent actions in another. Disease recognizes no political borders.

June 26, 2004 — The *Los Angeles Times* noted that a 71-year-old man became the first victim in Los Angeles County to contract the West Nile virus. The virus, which is typically carried by mosquitoes biting infected birds like crows, has been advancing across the country from the East Coast since 1999. The virus is not especially deadly, but it has killed almost 600 people across the United States since that time. The best defense is careful tracking of outbreaks, and then spraying with pesticides that kill the mosquitoes that spread the virus. As the name suggests, the origin of the virus is in Egypt. But in today's interconnected world, any disease in any place can ultimately show up in the United States, and public health officials have to plan accordingly.

July 2004 — A report issued this month by the Federal Interagency Forum on Child and Family Statistics showed that the birthrate among teenagers in the United States dropped to an all-time low in 2002, the latest year for which full statistics are available. The government has been keeping statistics on this issue since 1940. The birthrate dropped by 40 percent since 1991 for girls aged 15 to 17, and the rate for girls 18 and 19 also fell to historic lows. The biggest reductions were among black teenagers, and California had higher decreases than any other state.

For a variety of reasons, babies born by teenagers tend to have higher infant mortality rates, and so the reduction in teenage births is a positive step for overall public health. Experts credit an increase in more effective educational material directed at teenagers for the decrease in birthrates.

July 13, 2004—New guidelines for people at increased risk for heart disease or stroke that were developed by the National Cholesterol Education Program were published today in the journal *Circulation*. The key point of the new guidelines was that treatment with statin drugs should be intended to drive down LDL (bad cholesterol) levels to below 100 milligrams per deciliter rather than the higher 130 milligrams that had been the previous standard. In addition, the educational panel recommended an even lower standard of 70 milligrams for patients at very high risk (defined as persons with test results indicating the expectation of a heart attack within the next 10 years).

The more stringent recommendations are in recognition of the fact that about 42 percent of heart attack victims die within the first year of their attack. This makes it even more urgent to follow the protocol that prevention is far superior to trying to manage a disease after an event occurs. Many trials are underway in various parts of the world like the ones whose results led to the new guidelines. Thus, an additional round of new recommendations is expected in the near future.

The most widely used statin drug is Lipitor. As shown in the appendix, it is now the most often prescribed drug in the United States. But even with good discounts it is hard to reduce the drug's cost to less than a dollar a day, and this is another reason why there has been so much recent activity in making prescription drugs a covered portion of the Medicare program.

July 15, 2004—The Senate passed a measure today that would create a system to buy out tobacco farmers and give the Food and Drug Administration (FDA) authority to regulate certain aspects of tobacco production and cigarette manufacturing. The Senate measure would have to be reconciled with a similar House measure, and then be put into a form that the president would sign to become law. Thus, there are many steps to go, but at least some steps have been taken. The main focus of the measure would be to keep children from smoking. Senate members said that of the 40 million Americans who still smoke, about 90 percent said they started as children.

Senate members said simply making smoking illegal will not work. Prohibition of alcohol in 1919 proved that. Other senators said that local public bodies have had much more impact so far by outlawing smoking in public places. The buy-out is meant to correct problems created by the government in the 1930s by complicated quota and price support systems. But the key trade-off is to get the FDA the authority to regulate the industry, an authority the FDA attempted to impose in 1996, but one that the Supreme Court said the FDA did not have in 2000. This measure would fix that problem, and it might thus lead to federal control over cigarettes that would ultimately greatly reduce smoking even further in the United States.

July 16, 2004— The *Los Angeles Times* of this date carried an article stating that a new policy on obesity had been established by the Medicare program. Because obesity is now seen as a critical public health problem in the United States, Medicare officials were removing the statement that "obesity itself can not be considered an illness" from the Medicare manual. This will permit coverage for programs that cut obesity if the programs can "demonstrate their effectiveness" in improving the health of Medicare beneficiaries.

There are about 41 million people covered under the Medicare program, and 37 percent of them are considered overweight, with 18 percent falling into the category of "obese." But from 1991 to 1998, the prevalence of obesity among people aged 60 to 69 increased by 45 percent, according to the American Obesity Association. The new Medicare policy will not only permit certain programs addressing this issue to be eligible for Medicare payments, it should stimulate research programs to demonstrate the efficacy of various methods of reducing obesity.

July 19, 2004— The issue of *Time* with this date carried an article related to the 15th International AIDS Conference being held in Bangkok, Thailand. The host country had previously gained worldwide fame for educational/preventive programs that cut down the expected rate of new AIDS cases in the country, but a new United Nations report reported that Thailand, among many other countries, had been cutting back on preventative measures and that AIDS was on the rise again.

Ironically, the success of anti–AIDS drugs and the fact that people with AIDS are living longer has lulled many people into thinking that the AIDS crisis is easing. But it is estimated that as many as five million people were infected with the HIV virus in 2003, the most ever in a single year. About one-quarter of those new infections occurred in Asia, and new highs are believed to have occurred in China, Indonesia, and Vietnam. India is believed to have over 5 million people in total now infected with HIV, second only to South Africa in number of cases in the world. South African icon Nelson Mandela recently called for more international resources to be applied to tuberculosis on the basis that the basic final cause of death in many AIDS patients is tuberculosis, which readily attacks AIDS patients whose immune system is greatly weakened by their AIDS disease. The United Nations estimates that tuberculosis is responsible for as many as 40 percent of the 3 million AIDS deaths in Africa yearly.

The United Nations also cited AIDS as being responsible for reducing economic development and life expectancies in some countries. Zambia, where 16 percent of the population is infected with AIDS, has seen its life expectancy at birth drop to 32 years compared with 50 years three decades ago. The overall development ratings for 20 nations (13 of which are in Africa) have declined since 1990 due to AIDS.

Much controversy continues to surround the international effort to contain AIDS, both in terms of the basic causes of AIDS and the appropriate measures to combat those causes. In some places unsafe sex is the key problem, while in others the most intractable problem is intravenous drug use and sharing contaminated needles. Adding to the problems is the attitude certain governments take in preferring to pretend specific issues of one sort or another do not really exist in their country. AIDS on an international basis will not be easily controlled in many places.

In the United States, new AIDS cases numbered 42,475 in 2002 (down by about 40 percent from 1995 and down by almost 60 percent from their peak in the early 1990s). Annual deaths were 16,371 in 2002 (down by almost 70 percent both from 1995 and from their peak in the early 1990s). The number of new cases has remained relatively constant since the new century began, and the number of deaths continues to slowly decline on average. Since the AIDS epidemic started in earnest in the United States in 1985, about 57 percent of the new cases occurred in men having sex with men, 21 percent occurred among intravenous drug users, and about 8 percent occurred among men in both categories. Thus, the two categories of homosexual men and intravenous drug users accounted for about 86 percent of all new cases in men (which far outnumber new cases in women as shown in the appendix).

AIDS educational and preventative programs have basically kept AIDS constrained to these segments of the population, and educational programs and improved drugs have lowered the overall death rate of AIDS. The death rates are higher, of course, among the most typically affected populations, but compared to most of the rest of the world, AIDS overall is a disease that can be considered under control in the United States.

July 26, 2004— A report on malaria in the issue of *Time* magazine of this date shows that the old disease of malaria is now killing almost as many people (about 3 million yearly) as the new disease of AIDS. Worldwide, malaria death rates fell by almost 90 percent in the century between 1900 and 2000, but in Sub-Saharan Africa the death rate from malaria is almost back to the same level it reached in 1900. Malaria is a curable disease, but the problem in Africa is an all-too-common one for that country: not enough financial resources, outbreaks of violence, and governments hesitant to take bold steps.

In the United States, malaria (and yellow fever) are nearly now nonexistent. The more temperate climate helps, but continued mosquito eradication programs and new drug developments have essentially eliminated problems from these diseases. Lessons learned from finishing the Panama Canal helped to eliminate the breeding grounds of the mosquitoes, and DDT provided a final touch in the 1940s and 1950s. DDT helped get rid of the mosquitoes in many places in the world after World War II, and although DDT is now generally banned, exceptions are available for those African countries willing to seek them (much lower targeted application levels of DDT are now used effectively). Malaria parasites have developed drug resistance to many drugs, but there are other effective drugs available. They are still cheap by Western standards, but not by African standards.

Malaria is yet another deadly disease that has ravaged the world for many centuries, and still is doing so in many areas, but is generally nonexistent in the United States due to effective public health measures taken at the proper time and constant vigilance thereafter.

August 6, 2004— Updated statistics concerning the AIDS epidemic were contained today in an article in the *Los Angeles Times*. It was estimated that worldwide 20 million deaths from AIDS have occurred in the last 25 years. Presently, 38 million people in the world are infected with AIDS, 95 percent of them in third-world countries. The article concluded that much of the nearly $5 billion dollars being spent annually on AIDS (nearly two-thirds of which is donated by the United States) is being consumed by people who have a vested interest in maintaining their lucrative position in the AIDS bureaucracy, and too little is being spent trying to find a cure. The outlook is grim internationally for AIDS, and the record five million people infected last year is likely to be surpassed in the near future.

SUMMARY

The first effective step in public health that was based on an accurate scientific hypothesis was the vaccination process developed by Dr. Edward Jenner in England in 1796. His process was based on the use of a relatively harmless cowpox vaccine to prevent the deadly disease of smallpox. The process of vaccination gave mankind its first weapon against those microbes that cause infectious disease among the countless microbes with which we share the "ocean" of air everything on the planet lives in. Such vaccinations trigger the immune system of the human body to develop antibodies against infectious microbes whenever they invade on their own. The immune system has developed over the millions of years mammals and microbes have battled for supremacy on earth, and vaccination was the first technique found to artificially cause the immune system to go into its protective role.

The development of public health in the nineteenth century, after Jenner's work at the end of the eighteenth century, primarily concentrated on winning the battle against infectious disease. While scientists concentrated on finding the cause of infectious disease so they could develop more techniques to fight it (Jenner drew the correct hypothesis for his work but he knew nothing about the details of why it worked), a movement called the sanitarian movement became active. Sanitarians believed (incorrectly) that the cause of all disease was dirt and filth. They believed that miasmas (the smells and gas that arose from swamps and sewers and recently dug trenches) caused disease in some mysterious way. The sanitarians did a lot of good by clearing away dirt and filth (where many microbes resided) and lobbying for better water supplies and sewer systems, even if their belief about what caused disease was incorrect. Even when the germ theory of disease was well established by 1900, many sanitarians, including the famous Florence Nightingale, refused to change their beliefs.

The scientists of the later 1800s, led by the towering figure of Louis Pasteur, determined that specific microbes caused specific diseases, and then some new vaccines were slowly developed to fight these diseases. The flu/pneumonia pandemic of 1918–19 killed possibly 30 million people around the world, and demonstrated how essentially helpless mankind was against some diseases even if its cause was known. But soon chemotherapy in the form of antibiotics gave mankind a way to kill some previously deadly infectious diseases and bacteriological infections even after they were established in the body. The threat of infectious disease and infections was greatly reduced, at least in the United States.

The second half of the twentieth century, after Jonas Salk developed a successful vaccine against polio in 1954, saw the efforts of public health shift focus to the degenerative diseases of aging. The famous *Surgeon General's Report on Smoking and Health* in 1964 was indicative of this effort. Educational efforts were made to try to get people to make the changes in lifestyle that would help everyone to delay the onset of many chronic diseases.

Today, the United States resembles an island of good public health practices (and good health in general) in a sea of countries still suffering from old and new deadly diseases. Some other western and Asia-Pacific countries can match the United States in its efforts, but the gulf between the haves and have-nots continues to widen. With a gigantic public health service in terms of resources and technology, children in the United States have the benefit of a vaccine system that has essentially eliminated the deadly and crippling childhood diseases of only 50 to 75 years ago. Adult killer diseases like pneumonia, flu, tuberculosis, and syphilis have been reduced to statistical insignificance except in the elderly. Such natural diseases as cardiovascular disease, cancer, and stroke are now the big killers at nearly all ages above 25, and in spite of the effects of self-inflicted wounds like smoking and overeating, the overall death rates of these new killer diseases continue to decline (age-adjusted cancer death rates would show a notable decline if not for the number of females taking up smoking and dying of lung cancer).

A perhaps unnoticed effect of the public health system in the United States is its ability to track, classify, educated the public about, and ultimately isolate new diseases like hantavirus, Ebola virus, Legionnaire's disease, Lyme disease, toxic-shock syndrome, SARS, West Nile virus, and AIDS. Certainly the most notorious of these diseases is AIDS, but in the United States it has been relatively isolated among certain segments of the population. AIDS causes less than 1 percent of all deaths in the United States, and does not even make the top ten list of the causes of death. In other countries, especially Africa, ignorance, superstition, and corrupt political systems make AIDS a great killer that threatens to depopulate certain areas. A recent outbreak of polio in Africa was caused by the same reasons, and children are being crippled by a disease that has essentially disappeared in western countries. Successful public health requires the kind of ongoing organization changes and the shifting of resources that takes place regularly in the United States.

But having properly praised the status of public health in the United States, it must be noted that mankind and microbes are still locked in a deadly battle, and there is no assurance of the outcome. Microbes evolve just as mankind does, and the triumph of antibiotics at any given time only marks a pause in the battle. Old drugs eventually fail as microbes evolve into new forms, and new drugs are constantly needed. There still are no drugs to kill viruses, and how long current vaccines will work is unknown. If AIDS were spread by droplets in the air as people breathe instead of in the limited, difficult way it is by exchange of bodily fluids, AIDS, or a disease like it, could conceivably eliminate the human race before we learned how to stop it. The microbes appear to have been here for billions of years, and on that scale mankind is a relative newcomer on the scene. So the fundamental battle of technology versus microbes has to continue, apparently indefinitely. Public health can only disseminate what medical technology gives it, no matter how brilliantly organized the public health system is (and the United States is an example of the best the world has to offer).

APPENDIX 1:
DISEASE CAUSES OF DEATH
VERSUS ACTUAL CAUSES, 2000

Disease Causes of Death United States 2000	Percentage (of all deaths)	Actual Causes of Death United States 2000	Percentage (of all deaths)
Heart disease	30%	Tobacco	18.1%
Cancer	23%	Poor diet/Physical inactivity	16.6%
Stroke	7%	Alcohol consumption	3.5%
Chronic obstructive respiratory disease	5%	Microbial agents (e.g. influenza, pneumonia)	3.1%
Unintentional injuries	4%	Toxic agents (e.g. pollutants, asbestos)	2.3%
Diabetes	3%	Motor vehicles	1.8%
Pneumonia/influenza	3%	Firearms	1.2%
Alzheimer's disease	2%	Sexual behavior	0.8%
Kidney disease	2%	Illicit drug use	0.7%

The table above shows the top nine causes of death in the United States in the year 2000. Two different methods are used in showing the causes of death. The first column on the left shows the causes of death in the conventional manner, in terms of the disease that is deemed responsible for the death. The next column shows the percentage of all deaths caused by the specific disease. For example, heart disease caused 30 percent of all deaths in the United States in 2000, while kidney disease caused 2 percent.

The right two columns show the causes of death in the United States in the year 2000 in terms of the lifestyle choices that are believed to have caused the death. For example, the use of tobacco is estimated to have caused 18.1 percent of all deaths in the United States in 2000, while illicit drug use is estimated to have caused 0.7 percent.

Perhaps the most surprising thing about the table is the fact that while the use of tobacco ranks as the top lifestyle cause of death in the United States, poor diet and lack of physical activity ranks a very close second. Most people are aware that tobacco use causes many deaths in the United States, both from promoting many forms of cancer (especially lung cancer) and from causing cardiovascular diseases (especially heart disease) and respiratory diseases other than lung cancer. But many people are surprised to learn that poor diet and lack of physical activity taken together as a common cause produces nearly as many deaths as does the use of tobacco.

The combination of poor diet and lack of physical activity almost always results in obesity. This condition alone leads to much higher incidences of diabetes and high blood pressure, as well as increased strain and stress on the body as a whole and especially on the heart muscle. In addition, poor diet choices lead to a number of diseases, and a lack of physical activity produces poor heart function and a number of respiratory problems. The combination of poor diet and a lack of physical activity multiplies the effects of problems caused by one of the conditions by itself, and death arrives a little bit at a time, much ahead of its due date.

The top two lifestyle problems, tobacco use plus poor diet/lack of physical activity, account for 34.7 percent of all deaths. The third most deadly lifestyle problem, alcohol consumption, accounts for only 3.5 percent, or only a tenth of the deaths caused by the top two issues. In fact, all of the bottom seven of the top nine causes of death added together account for only 13.4 percent of all deaths, compared to 34.7 percent for the top two.

This means that such notorious issues as unsafe sexual behavior and illicit drug use (prime causes of AIDS and other diseases) account for only 1.5 percent of all deaths, while pollution in the worse case accounts for only 2.3 percent, and the tragic combination of motor-vehicle accidents and firearms combined account for only 3 percent. This is why so many public health officials point out that a substantial number of deaths in the United States are preventable, and that the basic lifestyle choices one makes have much more to do with death rates than issues that grab headlines such as AIDS or pollution or firearms.

It must be noted that this analysis is true only for the "good health island" of the United States, as discussed in the text of this book. Other countries, especially poorer ones, have many causes of death (like AIDS or other uncontrolled infectious diseases) that can overwhelm individual lifestyle choices. However, if there is one common lifestyle choice around the world that produces more deaths than any other, it is probably tobacco use. The United States is one of the leaders, if not the leader, in the world in attempting to curtail tobacco use on a national level.

Some countries, especially in Africa, have death rates from AIDS that far outweigh all other causes. But it is hard to say how much of this is due to lifestyle choices in the sense that an informed choice is being made. Where ignorance of the causes of a disease ranks as high as it does in places in Africa, one may not essentially choose to live in an unsafe manner. This is one reason that the United States public health system puts so much effort into educating the public about good health choices. One has to know about the implications of certain choices to make a truly informed decision. And the educational process has to take place in the context of the overall lifestyle of the country in which one lives. Trying to convince someone about the need for better diet and physical exercise choices if the person in question is living on a starvation diet and is exhausted every day from trying to stay alive is a hopeless project.

However, returning to the situation as it exists in the United States, it is clear that avoiding the use of tobacco and making careful choices about diet and physical activity will go a long way in the effort to avoid premature death. The prime causes of death in the United States are the degenerative diseases of aging. The rate of that degeneration can be reduced by specific lifestyle choices.

APPENDIX 2:
TEN LEADING CAUSES
OF DEATH, 1900–1940

Cause of Death	Rate	% of Total	Cause of Death	Rate	% of Total
1900			**1910**		
Pneumonia/Flu	202.2	11.8%	Heart Disease	158.9	10.8%
Tuberculosis	194.4	11.3%	Pneumonia/Flu	155.9	10.6%
Other Infectious[1]	186.7	10.9%	Tuberculosis	153.8	10.5%
Gastritis[2]	142.7	8.3%	Other Infectious	147.5	10.0%
Heart Disease	137.4	8.0%	Other CVD	117.2	8.0%
Stroke	106.9	6.2%	Gastritis	115.4	7.9%
Other CVD[3]	100.9	5.9%	Stroke	95.8	6.5%
Accidents	72.3	4.2%	Accident	84.2	5.7%
Cancer	64.0	3.7%	Cancer	76.2	5.2%
Perinatal[4]	62.6	3.6%	Perinatal	73.0	5.0%
1918			**1920**		
Pneumonia/Flu	588.5	32.5%	Pneumonia/Flu	207.3	16.0%
Heart Disease	171.6	9.5%	Heart Disease	159.6	12.3%
Tuberculosis	149.8	8.3%	Tuberculosis	113.1	8.7%
Other CVD	121.4	6.7%	Other CVD	112.3	8.6%
Other Infectious	116.9	6.5%	Other Infectious	103.0	7.9%
Stroke	94.0	5.2%	Stroke	93.0	7.2%
Accidents	81.5	4.5%	Cancer	83.4	6.4%
Cancer	80.8	4.5%	Accidents	70.0	5.4%

1. *Other infectious disease includes respiratory infections, syphilis, acute nephritis, diphtheria, typhoid, whooping cough, measles, scarlet fever, streptococcal sore throat, and (after 1930) gastritis.*
2. *Gastritis includes diarrhea, enteritis, and colitis.*
3. *Other CVD includes all cardiovascular diseases other than heart disease and stroke.*
4. *Perinatal problems originate between the 28th week of pregnancy and 28 days after birth.*

Cause of Death	Rate	% of Total	Cause of Death	Rate	% of Total
1918			**1920**		
Gastritis	75.2	4.0%	Perinatal	69.2	5.3%
Perinatal	70.0	3.9%	Gastritis	53.7	4.1%
1930			**1940**		
Heart Disease	214.2	18.9%	Heart Disease	292.5	27.2%
Other CVD	111.2	9.8%	Cancer	120.3	11.2%
Pneumonia/Flu	102.5	9.1%	Other CVD	102.3	9.5%
Cancer	97.4	8.6%	Stroke	90.9	8.4%
Stroke	89.0	7.9%	Accidents	73.2	6.8%
Accidents	79.8	7.0%	Pneumonia/Flu	70.3	6.5%
Tuberculosis	71.1	6.3%	Other Infectious	55.6	5.2%
Other Infectious	59.5	5.3%	Tuberculosis	45.9	4.3%
Perinatal	49.6	4.4%	Perinatal	39.2	3.6%
Gastritis	26.0	2.3%	Diabetes	26.6	2.5%

The preceding tables show the ten leading causes of death from 1900 through 1940, by decade, and for 1918 (a year with an unusually high number of deaths due to the global flu epidemic of 1918–1919). The tables show the death rate per 100,000 and the percentage of total deaths resulting from each cause.

The major infectious diseases from 1900 through 1940 were pneumonia/flu, tuberculosis, and, up to 1930, gastritis (which combines the main infectious diseases of the digestive tract and which was a major killer of infants and children). After 1930, gastritis is included in the broad term "other infectious diseases" which include the familiar diseases shown in the first footnote. The four broad causes of death from 1900 through 1940 were infectious diseases, cardiovascular diseases, cancer, and accidents. Perinatal, the other major cause shown, includes certain disease originating in the perinatal period, which only affect infants as indicated in footnote four.

Pneumonia/flu and tuberculosis were at the top of the causes of death list in 1900, with heart disease fifth and cancer ninth. Heart disease rose to first by 1910 and remained there until the flu epidemic of 1918-1919 killed 558.5 people per 100,000 in 1918 (the 558.5 rate is by far the highest death rate of the century for a single cause in a single year). The residual effect of the epidemic left pneumonia/flu at the top in 1920, with tuberculosis third in 1910, 1918, and 1920 (tuberculosis was in first place six times before 1910). The combination of these diseases is why infectious diseases were considered the top killers in the United States through 1920.

As discussed in the text, improved public health actions in sanitation, nutrition, and health care (including the development of some vaccines) drove infectious diseases down the death list well before the general use of antibiotics in the 1940s. The development of the germ theory of disease prior to

1900 was also a major factor in reducing deaths from infectious diseases by making it possibly to identify the specific bacteria that caused the diseases and to screen for their elimination from the water and food supply.

By 1940, pneumonia/flu was only the sixth leading cause of death, and tuberculosis had fallen to the eighth spot in the top ten causes of death. The combined death rate of these two diseases in 1940 was 116.2 per 100,000, which was a 71 percent reduction from a combined rate of 396.6 per 100,000 in 1900. Total infectious diseases of all kinds on the list fell by 76 percent between 1900 and 1940. This is why the claim is made that infectious disease had essentially been conquered by public health initiatives before the dawn of the age of antibiotics.

Heart disease reclaimed the top spot among the ten biggest causes of death by 1921, and it never relinquished its first-place position again. Thus, heart disease was the top killer in 1930 with "other cardiovascular diseases" in second place and cancer in fourth place. By 1940, cancer was second with stroke in fourth place. Heart disease and cancer have remained the top two killers in the United States every year since 1940 (stroke moved to third in 1950, and these three diseases have not changed position since).

Other cardiovascular diseases steadily moved down the list after 1940, because better and better treatments were found for these diseases over the decades. But heart disease in its most dramatic form is essentially a heart attack that can cause instant death. So far no treatment has been found to fix this particular condition. When your heart, for whatever reason, goes into fibrillation and stops pumping blood (or if a heart in congestive heart failure simply stops during sleep), the result is death (unless someone is nearby to get the heart pumping again practically instantaneously). Thus, although "other cardiovascular diseases" are subject to intervention by continual medical developments, death as a result of a heart attack or another form of sudden cardiac arrest is essentially as final as anything can be.

Except for pneumonia/flu in 1918 and in 1920, heart disease was the only leading cause of death to account for more than 12 percent of all deaths in the first two decades of the 1900s. The top leading infectious cause of death accounted for only 11.8 percent and 10.6 percent of all deaths in 1900 and 1910 respectively, jumped to a then-phenomenal 32.5 percent in 1918 at the peak of the flu epidemic, and fell to 16 percent as the epidemic ebbed in 1920. But heart disease caused 18.9 percent of all deaths in 1930 and climbed to 27.2 percent in 1940. As will be shown in Appendix 3, deaths due to heart disease rose to over 38 percents of all deaths from 1960 through 1980. In this sense, heart disease caused an epidemic of its own. In spite of the greater notoriety of infectious diseases in the early part of the twentieth century, heart disease has been a great killer in the United States for over 100 years.

One reason heart disease claims such a high percentage of all deaths is the fact that other reasons for death were declining (other than cancer) as the century went on. But heart disease as a great killer has been with us almost as long as the United States has been a country, contrary to the perception of many that heart disease is a modern disease caused by the stresses and strains of our modern times.

Actually, the manner in which the body functions makes the heart a highly likely cause of death. The system to carry sustaining blood to the heart muscle is fraught with many potential blockages, and to some extent, a heart attack is an accident waiting to happen. If the heart were able to draw the blood it needs from the blood flowing through it (all the blood in the body ultimately flows through the heart), then we would never hear about such things as infarctions and blood clots and "plumbing" accidents that produce death. But the pumping system with the heart at its center delivering blood through arteries subject to clogging is not designed for long-term use. Thus, it should be expected that heart disease would be the major cause of death around the world. Essentially as soon as infectious diseases were, to some degree, conquered in the United States, heart disease rose immediately to the top of the causes of death, and it has stayed there.

Diabetes made the list of the top ten killers in 1940, partly because the decline of infectious diseases reduced the death rate level needed to make the top ten list. This type of effect became even more pronounced in the United States after 1940. But diabetes has been a continual important cause of death in the second half of the twentieth century, and it rose to sixth place on the list by 2000.

APPENDIX 3:
TEN LEADING CAUSES
OF DEATH, 1950–2000

Cause of Death	Rate	% of Total	Cause of Death	Rate	% of Total
1950			**1960**		
Heart Disease	356.8	37.0%	Heart Disease	369.0	38.7%
Cancer	139.8	14.5%	Cancer	149.2	15.6%
Stroke	104.0	10.8%	Stroke	108.0	11.3%
Accidents	60.6	6.3%	Accidents	52.3	5.5%
Perinatal[1]	40.5	4.2%	Other CVD	38.1	4.0%
Other CVD[2]	33.6	3.5%	Perinatal	37.4	3.9%
Pneumonia/Flu	31.3	3.2%	Pneumonia/Flu	37.3	3.9%
Other Infectious[3]	30.8	3.2%	Other Infectious	32.2	3.4%
Tuberculosis	22.5	2.3%	Diabetes	16.7	1.7%
Diabetes	16.2	1.7%	Congenital[4]	12.2	1.3%
1970			**1980**		
Heart Disease	362.0	38.3%	Heart Disease	336.0	38.3%
Cancer	162.8	17.2%	Cancer	183.9	20.9%
Stroke	101.9	10.8%	Stroke	75.1	8.6%
Accidents	56.4	6.0%	Accidents	46.7	5.3%
Other CVD	32.1	3.4%	Other CVD	25.3	2.9%
Pneumonia/Flu	30.9	3.3%	COPD[5]	24.7	2.9%
Perinatal	21.3	2.3%	Pneumonia/Flu	24.1	2.7%
Diabetes	18.9	2.0%	Diabetes	15.4	1.8%

1. *Perinatal problems originate between the 28th week of pregnancy and 28 days after birth.*
2. *Other CVD includes all cardiovascular disease other than heart disease and stroke.*
3. *Other infectious diseases includes those shown in Appendix 2. In 1990 it also includes HIV/AIDS.*
4. *Congenital deaths are due to malformations and anomalies present at birth.*
5. *COPD (chronic obstructive pulmonary diseases) includes bronchitis, emphysema, and asthma.*

Cause of Death	Rate	% of Total	Cause of Death	Rate	% of Total
1970			**1980**		
Liver Disease	15.5	1.6%	Liver Disease	13.5	1.5%
COPD[5]	15.2	1.6%	Suicide	11.9	1.4%
1990			**2000**		
Heart Disease	289.5	33.5%	Heart Disease	258.2	29.6%
Cancer	203.2	23.5%	Cancer	200.9	23.0%
Stroke	57.9	6.7%	Stroke	60.9	7.0%
Accidents	37.0	4.3%	COPD	44.3	5.1%
COPD	34.9	4.0%	Accidents	35.6	4.1%
Pneumonia/Flu	32.0	3.7%	Diabetes	25.2	2.9%
Other CVD	20.9	2.4%	Pneumonia/Flu	23.7	2.7%
Diabetes	19.2	2.2%	Alzheimer's	18.0	2.1%
Other Infectious	15.2	1.8%	Kidney Disease	13.5	1.5%
Suicide	12.4	1.4%	Blood Poisoning	11.3	1.3%

The preceding tables show the top ten leading causes of death from 1950 through 2000 by decade, with 2000 being selected as the most recent year to keep each individual table separated by an even ten years. The tables show the death rate per 100,000 people and the percentage of total deaths resulting from each cause.

Heart disease, cancer, stroke, and accidents — in that order — occupy the top four places on each list from 1950 to 1990. In 2000, chronic obstructive pulmonary diseases (COPD) replaced accidents in fourth place. There are additional changes farther down the list, because the top four causes accounted for such a high percentage of total deaths that other items had relatively small percentages. Thus, a relatively small change from decade to decade would determine whether different causes made the list.

Heart disease accounted for a nearly constant percentage of deaths from 1950 through 1980 (37, 38.7, 38.3, and 38.3 percent respectively). The percentage declined to 33.5 percent in 1990 and 29.6 percent in 2000. The absolute death rate fell from a peak of 369 in 1960 to 258.2 in 2000, a drop of 30 percent. The rate is still slowly falling today. It's an excellent example of how positive changes in lifestyle can affect death rates (together with improvements in medical treatment).

The changes in death rates for cancer also serve as an excellent example of how changes in lifestyle can affect death rates, but this time the relationship has a negative result. The death rate for cancer increased steadily from 1950 through 1990, with a small decline between 1990 and 2000. The percentage of total deaths accounted for by cancer increased from 14.5 percent in 1950 to 23.5 percent in 1990 and then dropped slightly to 23 percent in 2000. This is a net increase of 59 percent from 1950 to 2000. The increase in cancer deaths is due entirely to increases in deaths from lung cancer caused by smoking.

For both men and women, most cancer death rates since 1950 have declined (sometimes substantially) or remained nearly the same for all sites in the body except for the lungs and the related thoracic area. For men, the age-adjusted death rate for lung cancer began to slow near the end of the twentieth century, but the increase in smoking by women after 1950 is now producing dramatic increases in lung cancer for women. Breast cancer gets much more publicity, but lung cancer kills many more women than breast cancer and has done so since the mid–1980s.

Thus, although cancer has become one of the most dreaded diseases during the second half of the twentieth century, almost all forms of cancer are either in decline or nearly constant. If people had never taken up smoking, cancer would still be the second-leading killer behind heart disease, but it would be much further behind than it is and probably a much-less feared disease. Over half of all cancer deaths are clearly the result of a self-inflicted wound caused by smoking. Men have died from lung cancer in large numbers since 1950, but, as noted before, in recent decades the death rate for lung cancer in men has begun to level off as they discontinue smoking. But unfortunately, women — especially young adults — have taken up the habit in a dramatic fashion, and lung cancer deaths in women are still climbing rapidly.

The overall result is that heart disease and cancer far outweigh all other causes of death in the United States. In 1950, they combined for 51.5 percent of all deaths; in 2000, they combined for 52.6 percent of all deaths. The 2000 level is at least well below the combined peak of 59.2 percent in 1980, but almost all of the decline can be credited to the decline in heart disease. No other cause of death comes close to these two. Stroke, in third place in 2000 (as it has been since 1950), accounted for only 7 percent of all deaths.

Even the epidemic of HIV/AIDS accounted for only 1.6 percent of all deaths at its peak in the early 1990s, and deaths due to AIDS have since fallen off the list of the top ten causes of death in the United States. The relative importance of other causes of death is quite different for different age groups, but on an overall basis, the main causes of death in the United States are heart disease and cancer. Other causes may at times have higher rates of increase, but it will be a very long time before they account for a significant portion of deaths in this country.

The information in Appendix 1 shows quite clearly that premature death can be avoided if people changed their basic lifestyles. This includes, of course, stopping smoking, but poor diet and lack of physical exercise greatly increase the likelihood of heart disease. Tobacco use directly produces the single largest cause of cancer deaths, lung cancer. So the conclusion is once again drawn that, given the primary causes of death in the United States are due to degenerative diseases of aging, the rate of that degeneration could be significantly reduced by more careful choices of lifestyle.

APPENDIX 4:
TEN LEADING CAUSES
OF DEATH, 1900–2000

Cause of Death	Rate	% of Total	Cause of Death	Rate	% of Total
1900			**1918**		
Pneumonia/Flu	202.2	11.8%	Pneumonia/Flu	588.5	32.5%
Tuberculosis	194.4	11.3%	Heart Disease	171.6	9.5%
Other Infectious[1]	186.7	10.9%	Tuberculosis	149.8	8.3%
Gastritis	142.7	8.3%	Other CVD	121.4	6.7%
Heart Disease	137.4	8.0%	Other Infectious	116.9	6.5%
Stroke	106.9	6.2%	Stroke	94.0	5.2%
Other CVD[2]	100.9	5.9%	Accidents	81.5	4.5%
Accidents	72.3	4.2%	Cancer	80.8	4.5%
Cancer	64.0	3.7%	Gastritis	75.2	4.0%
Perinatal[3]	62.6	3.6%	Perinatal	70.0	3.9%
1940			**1960**		
Heart Disease	292.5	27.2%	Heart Disease	369.0	38.7%
Cancer	120.3	11.2%	Cancer	149.2	15.6%
Other CVD	102.3	9.5%	Stroke	108.0	11.3%
Stroke	90.9	8.4%	Accidents	52.3	5.5%
Accidents	73.2	6.8%	Other CVD	38.1	4.0%
Pneumonia/Flu	70.3	6.5%	Perinatal	37.4	3.9%
Other Infectious	55.6	5.2%	Pneumonia/Flu	37.3	3.9%
Tuberculosis	45.9	4.3%	Other Infectious	32.2	3.4%
Perinatal	39.2	3.6%	Diabetes	16.7	1.7%
Diabetes	26.6	2.5%	Congenital[4]	12.2	1.3%

1. Other infectious diseases and gastritis are explained in Appendices 2 and 3.
2. Other CVD includes all cardiovascular diseases other than heart disease and stroke.
3. Perinatal problems originate between the 28th week of pregnancy and 28 days after birth.
4. Congenital deaths are due to malformations and anomalies present at birth.

Cause of Death	Rate	% of Total	Cause of Death	Rate	% of Total
1980			**2000**		
Heart Disease	336.0	38.3%	Heart Disease	258.2	29.6%
Cancer	183.9	20.9%	Cancer	200.9	23.0%
Stroke	75.1	8.6%	Stroke	60.9	7.0%
Accidents	46.7	5.3%	COPD	44.3	5.1%
Other CVD	25.3	2.9%	Accidents	35.6	4.1%
COPD[5]	24.7	2.9%	Diabetes	25.2	2.9%
Pneumonia/Flu	24.1	2.7%	Pneumonia/Flu	23.7	2.7%
Diabetes	15.4	1.8%	Alzheimer's	18.0	2.1%
Liver Disease	13.5	1.5%	Kidney Disease	13.5	1.5%
Suicide	11.9	1.4%	Blood Poisoning	11.3	1.3%

The tables above show the ten leading causes of death for 1900, 1918, 1940, 1960, 1980, and 2000. This is approximately every 20 years during the twentieth century, with 1918 being selected because of the global flu epidemic of 1918. Appendix 4 supplements the data in appendices 2 and 3 by showing the changes in causes of death over the full century compared in one figure. This gives added perspective to the manner in which the leading causes of death change from the beginning of the twentieth century to the end.

Infectious diseases were the primary cause of death for the first two decades of the twentieth century. Pneumonia/flu tops the list for 1900 and 1918, with tuberculosis and other infectious diseases not far behind. The total deaths from infectious diseases of all types accounted for 42.2 percent of all deaths in 1900 and 51.2 percent in 1918. The 51.2 percent for 1918 was the peak for infectious diseases in the century, and by the early 1920s, infectious diseases were no longer the leading cause of death in the United States. This was well before the advent of antibiotic drugs in the 1930s and 1940s. The decline in the death rates due to infectious diseases prior to the coming of antibiotic drugs was due to great improvements in sanitation and the development of various vaccines as described in this book.

The first time heart disease and cancer were the leading two causes of death was in 1940. These two diseases accounted for 38.4 percent of all deaths in 1940, but total cardiovascular disease (heart disease, stroke, and other cardiovascular diseases) accounted for 45.1 percent in 1940. By 1960, total cardiovascular diseases accounted for 54 percent of all deaths, topping the 51.2 percent peak for infectious diseases in 1918. Cardiovascular diseases were at their peak in 1960, and together with cancer they accounted for 69.6 percent of all deaths that year.

By 1980, cardiovascular diseases had declined to 49.8 percent of all

---

5. COPD (chronic obstructive pulmonary diseases) includes bronchitis, emphysema, and asthma.

deaths, but the combination of cardiovascular diseases and cancer accounted for 70.7 percent of all deaths. The peak year for deaths was 1980 due to the combination of cardiovascular diseases of all types and cancer. In 2000, total cardiovascular diseases of all types fell to 38 percent of all deaths, and the combination of cancer and cardiovascular diseases fell to 61 percent of all deaths. This decline came in spite of a 12 percent increase in the percentage of deaths caused by cancer between 1980 and 2000.

Thus, the combination of cardiovascular diseases and cancer has been the prime cause of death in the United States in the second half of the twentieth century. There are many other disease processes that affect the constantly aging population of the United States, but for all practical purposes, these diseases are statistically very minor compared to cardiovascular diseases and cancer. That is why so many public health resources are assigned to these diseases.

Accidents were the next leading cause of death during the century behind cardiovascular diseases, infectious diseases, and cancer. In spite of the increasing toll of motor vehicle deaths during the century, accidents peaked in terms of percentage of total deaths at 7 percent in 1930. In 1940 they were close to this peak at 6.8 percent. But by 2000, they accounted for only 4.1 percent of all deaths, a decline of over 40 percent from the 7 percent peak in 1940. The United States has consistently become a safer place to work and play since 1930, in spite of the dramatically higher number of cars and trucks on the road.

If we combine the number of deaths caused by accidents with the number of deaths caused by homicide and suicide, we can create a category called "violent" deaths. In spite of perceptions that this category has been growing steadily during the twentieth century, it has actually changed relatively little over the full century. The peak years for violent deaths occurred in the 1930s, due to the combination of lawlessness and suicides during the Great Depression. There has been much notoriety near the end of the twentieth century about gang killings and associated forms of homicide in the big cities of the United States, but this activity, however deplorable, has not caused violent deaths to greatly exceed levels recorded earlier in the century.

APPENDIX 5:
DEATH RATES PER 100,000
FOR SELECTED CAUSES,
1900–2000

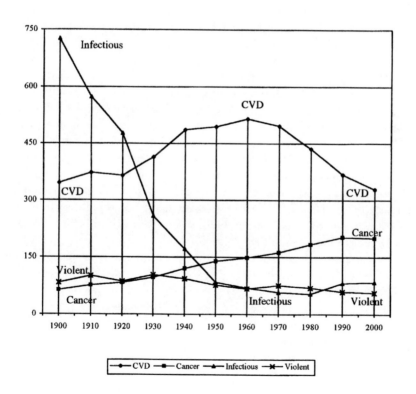

Year	CVD	Cancer	Infectious	Violent
1900	345.2	64.0	726.0	83.7
1910	371.9	76.2	572.6	104.1
1920	364.9	83.4	477.1	87.0
1930	414.4	97.4	259.1	104.3
1940	485.7	120.3	171.8	93.9
1950	494.4	139.8	84.6	77.3
1960	515.1	149.2	69.5	67.6
1970	496.0	162.8	58.2	76.3
1980	436.4	183.9	54.1	69.3
1990	368.3	203.2	82.1	59.4
2000	329.1	200.9	84.3	56.6

The graph on page 145 combines causes of death into four large categories. These categories are: cardiovascular diseases, cancer, infectious diseases, and violent deaths. Essentially, the causes of death in the United States during the twentieth century can be combined and compared in just these four categories, regardless of the many individual causes of death.

Cardiovascular diseases include heart disease, stroke, and various other cardiovascular diseases. Infectious diseases include pneumonia/flu, tuberculosis, chronic obstructive pulmonary disease (COPD, even if not strictly infectious), and the many other infectious diseases previously identified in this book. This category encompasses nearly every infectious disease known to the general public, including HIV/AIDS. The violent category includes accidents of all types, suicide, and homicide. Cancer actually includes many different types of cancer that occur at many different sites in the body, but most physicians generally accept that the word "cancer" actually includes a number of individual forms of the disease.

Infectious diseases were the leading cause of death from 1900 through the early 1920s. They had a death rate more than twice as high as cardiovascular diseases in 1900, and even in 1920, the death rate of infectious diseases was 31 percent higher than that of cardiovascular diseases. But by 1930, cardiovascular diseases had a death rate 60 percent higher than that of infectious disease. By 1960, the death rate for cardiovascular diseases was 7.4 times as high as that as infectious diseases. From 1960 through 2000, the cardiovascular disease death rate fell by more than 30 percent, while the rate for infectious diseases increased by about 56 percent between 1980 and 2000 as immigration and drug-resistant strains and new diseases like AIDS increased the problem of infectious diseases. In spite of these opposing trends, the death rate for cardiovascular diseases was still about four times as high as that for infectious diseases in 2000.

Cancer had the lowest death rate of the four groups in 1900, and the death rate for cancer did not catch up to the death rate of violent deaths until the early 1930s. Cancer moved into second place among the leading causes of death in the middle of the 1940s, when the death rate for cancer passed that of infectious diseases for the first time. Cancer was continuing a constant, upward climb at the time, while the infectious disease death rate was falling sharply. In 1950, the death rate for cancer was 65 percent higher than the death rate for infectious diseases and 81 percent higher than the rate for violent deaths. The death rate for cancer increased in every decade during the twentieth century through 1990. By 2000, it was more than three times as high as it had been in 1900.

Cardiovascular diseases, on the other hand, had an absolute death rate in 2000 that was actually lower than in 1900. This is because that although heart disease/heart attacks had increased during the century due to the aging of the population, other cardiovascular diseases had decreased dramatically due to better knowledge of how to care for such diseases and how to prevent them. As a separate disease category, "other" cardiovascular diseases fell from a death rate of over 100 in 1900 to about 10 in 2000. This drop, plus a smaller reduction in strokes, offset the increase in heart disease during the century and produced a net reduction in the category of total cardiovascular disease during the twentieth century.

The death rate from violent deaths was more than 30 percent lower in 2000 than in 1900. Infectious diseases were 87 percent lower in 2000 than in 1900. Thus, cancer was the only leading cause of death to increase significantly during the century. The substantial increase in cancer deaths is entirely due to a substantial increase in lung cancer deaths due to smoking. Nearly all other kinds of cancer deaths have either decreased since the 1940s or remained substantially the same. In essence, cancer is a disease generally under control in the United States. Lung cancer, which in many respects is a self-inflicted wound, is an exception.

The death rate for violent deaths was relatively flat from 1900 through 1940, growing from a level of 83.7 in 1900 to 93.9 per 100,000 in 1940. The peak was near 104 in 1910 and 1930. The death rate for violent deaths fell after 1940, with only a small increase occurring between 1960 and 1970, interrupting a steady decline from 1930 through 2000. But the pattern for the three components of violent deaths (accidents, suicide, homicide) each varied in a different way. The accident death rate slowly declined during the century, the suicide rate remained nearly constant, and the homicide rate increased somewhat. But total "violent" deaths show that the United States was a much safer place in 2000 than in 1900.

APPENDIX 6:
DISCOVERY OF
DISEASE ORGANISMS

Year	Disease Organism	Investigator
1879	Gonorrhea	Neisser
1880	Typhoid (bacillus found)	Eberth
	Leprosy	Hansen
	Malaria	Laveran
1882	Tuberculosis	Koch
	Glanders	Loeffler and Schutz
1883	Cholera	Koch
	Streptococcus (erysipelas)	Fehleisen
1884	Diphtheria	Kleps and Loeffler
	Typhoid (bacillus isolated)	Gaffky
	Staphylococcus	Rosenbach
	Streptococcus	Rosenbach
	Tetanus	Nicolaier
1885	Coli	Escherich
1886	Pneumococcus	A. Fraenkel
1887	Malta fever	Bruce
	Soft chancre	Ducrey
1892	Gas gangrene	Welch and Nuttall
1894	Plague	Yersin, Kitasato
	Botulism	van Ermengem
1898	Dysentery bacillus	Shiga

The preceding table shows the chronology in which the various bacteria causing specific infectious diseases were discovered at the end of the nineteenth century, when the germ theory of disease became firmly established. This revolutionized both medicine and public health. The table shows the year the discovery was made, the name of the disease caused by the bacteria that was isolated, and the name of the person or persons who made the discovery. Almost none of the names of the persons making the discovery, except perhaps for Koch, will be recognized by people outside the field of medicine or public health. It takes many people to make a revolution, and many of them remain anonymous to outsiders.

Many people were, in fact, at work in the field in the second half of the nineteenth century, led by Louis Pasteur, in the search for the causes of infectious diseases. They collectively had to throw out the concept that such diseases arose via spontaneous generation (a concept Pasteur demolished with an elegant demonstration in 1864). When Pasteur developed the concept of what became known as pasteurization in 1862, a process in which he stopped the souring of wine by heating it to 135 degrees Fahrenheit to destroy the bacteria he had identified under the microscope that caused the fermentation process to go wrong, it started a small revolution on its own. Doctors and scientists recognized that Pasteur had indeed proven what would become the germ theory of disease. Now that they knew the bacteria were out there, they tried to emulate Pasteur by finding the particular bacteria that produced a given disease.

The table might make it appear as if the discoveries all happened neatly in order, but what actually took place was that years of study began to come to fruition at nearly the same time. The details of each discovery did aid each next discovery in an iterative fashion. Louis Pasteur got the ball rolling with his discovery of pasteurization and his work in developing a vaccine (named in honor of his personal hero Dr. Edward Jenner of smallpox fame) for chicken cholera in 1879. Pasteur then developed an anthrax vaccine for animals in 1881 and silenced his veterinarian belittlers by conducting a public demonstration in which a number of animals were given a deadly dose of anthrax after some were vaccinated and some were not. When every vaccinated animal survived and every non-vaccinated animal died, the veterinarians stopped laughing and rushed off to answer the requests of farmers to vaccinate thousands of animals in an area around Paris. Pasteur's coup de grâce was curing a young boy who had been bitten by a rabid dog in 1885, a happening that had always previously been a death sentence. Pasteur's rabies vaccine (it was actually a cure rather than a preventive vaccine) brought him worldwide attention.

Pasteur's huge shadow hung over all the discoveries listed in the table, because it was hoped that each discovery would be followed by a preventive vaccine like those developed by Pasteur. This was especially true of Robert Koch's isolation of the bacteria that causes tuberculosis in 1882. Tuberculosis was one of mankind's biggest killers at the time, and a vaccine would potentially save millions of lives. Koch's discovery caused a sensation of its own around the world because of this fervent hope. However, almost none of the discoveries listed in the table resulted immediately in a vaccine. It would take many years for this to happen.

In the case of tuberculosis, a BCG vaccine (named after the initials of the last names of its developers, Bacillus Calmette-Guerin) was developed in 1906 by Messieurs Calmette and Guerin of the Pasteur Institute in Paris but not released for general use until 1921. It remained controversial as to its effectiveness for decades afterward. It was not until 1944 when the antibiotic streptomycin, developed specifically for tuberculosis by Selman Waksman, came on the scene that tuberculosis could be eliminated as a killer with no cure.

Other vaccines were available in the first decade of the twentieth century, but one of the few that was unquestionably effective was the vaccine developed for diphtheria. It started out as an antitoxin that would cure diphtheria after it was discovered that the killing effects of diphtheria were due to toxins produced by the bacteria rather than the bacteria per se. This led eventually to a true preventive vaccine, thanks in no small part to the work done by William H. Park and his associates at the New York City Board of Health. Their vaccine for diphtheria became part of the DPT vaccine that saved millions of lives among children in the early twentieth century and is still saving them today.

But even if the anticipated rush of vaccines did not take place right away, a key benefit of the list of discoveries was the knowledge of the causative factors of the diseases as well as the understanding of the manner in which the diseases could be spread. These factors alone caused a revolution in public health actions. Using tuberculosis again as an example, knowing the causative factor of the disease and learning that it was spread by air droplets from those infected, led to curative techniques such as sanitariums and the appropriate isolation of victims to control the spread of the disease. Tuberculosis death rates had been falling for decades when the antibiotic streptomycin was developed in the 1940s.

Further, knowing how to identify the bacteria that caused tuberculosis led to screening techniques that would remove it from the food supply, especially milk. The same sort of screening techniques were developed to avoid other bacteria that could be in the water and milk supply. Being able to remove these bacteria saved the lives of many infants and toddlers who otherwise would have developed gastrointestinal infections and suffered from the severe diarrhea that was often fatal to them.

Some names not on the list must be given credit for providing an environment in which the discoveries could be made and for providing techniques like staining bacteria so they could more easily be seen and identified. Names that should be noted in addition to those in the table include Ferdinand Cohn, a German naturalist and botanist who was regarded as the leading bacteriologist of his day. Cohn provided the first forum for Robert Koch to describe his work, and Cohn was a prime supporter of Koch and many others in establishing the germ theory of disease. Paul Ehrlich is another important person who developed early methods of staining bacteria so they could be clearly seen under the microscope. Ehrlich was an assistant to Koch. When Ehrlich began to study immunology, he essentially created a new field of study. Ehrlich worked intensively in the toxin area that ultimately led to the development of a vaccine for diphtheria, among other things. Ehrlich also was essentially the first to develop the field of chemotherapy and antibiotics, and in the early 1900s he came up with salvarsan as a magic bullet to destroy syphilis. Cohn and Ehrlich made key contributions to the fields that helped those listed in the table to make their discoveries.

An ironic result of the development of the germ theory of disease was that certain sanitarians, such as the famous Florence Nightingale, refused to accept the theory. She believed until her death in 1910 that dirt and filth were the causes of disease. She believed there was only one basic state of disease that expressed itself in many ways, depending on the degree of dirt and filth and crowding that was present. Actually, the germ theory of disease created a rationale for how a disease was started and how it spread in filthy, unsanitary conditions, but Nightingale refused to vary from her position. This attitude, expressed in similar ways by many scientists and physicians, was one reason why vaccines did not follow immediately from the discoveries in the table. As has always been the case, a new way of looking at things, no matter how rational, takes time to be widely accepted.

APPENDIX 7:
1918 INFLUENZA AND PNEUMONIA DEATHS

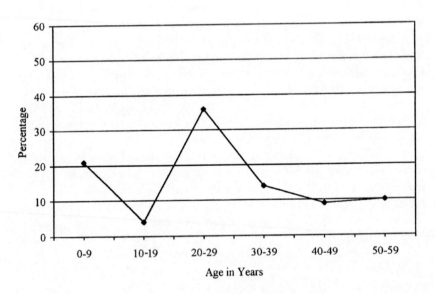

Age	Percent
0–9	21
10–19	4
20–29	36
30–39	14
40–49	9
50–59	10

The preceding graph shows an example of a W curve such as that obtained when the percentage of deaths suffered by various age groups in the worldwide flu/pneumonia pandemic of 1918 are plotted as shown, with the percentage of deaths listed on the Y axis and the different age groups listed on the X axis. A normal curve of this type would have a U shape, meaning that the highest percentage of deaths would occur among the youngest and oldest age groups.

Many diseases produce a U shape when the percentage of deaths in each age group are plotted in the way shown in the figure, because the very young and very old are most vulnerable to infectious disease, especially the flu and its complications. In fact, a mortality curve in the absence of a specific disease would have a U shape because death rates are almost always greater among the very young and the very old.

One of the great mysteries of the flu/pneumonia pandemic of 1918–19 is why the disease was so deadly among young adults in what should have been the prime of their life. In the figure, the percentage of deaths in the 20–29 age group is about 75 percent higher than in the 0–9 age group, and the percentage of deaths in the age 20–29 group remains more than three times higher than in any older age groups up to the 60–69 age group. Unfortunately, no one has been able to specifically define why this effect took place. In the 85 years that have passed since the pandemic ended, no one has also been able to answer the question of why the pandemic was so deadly in general. In that sense we cannot be sure if we can respond more effectively today to a similar pandemic than we did in 1918. However, there are some reasonable theories about the answers to these questions; if they are correct, we might make a better response the next time around.

First, it is thought the flu/pneumonia epidemic of 1918–19 might better be described as a pneumonia epidemic, because it is generally believed than pneumonia did the majority of the killing after the attack of the flu left the victim weak and subject to a deadly attack of pneumonia (and other infectious diseases). Viruses could not be seen in 1918 and relatively little was known about them. The bacteria called Pfeiffer's bacillus, after the man who discovered it in the 1890s, was believed to be the main cause of the killer pneumonia in 1918, and the bacillus did in fact have a long association with cases of flu that produced pneumonia (for a time the bacillus was thought to be the cause of flu itself until it was finally discovered that flu was caused by a virus). Some researchers felt there was a symbiotic relationship between flu and the bacillus, and when the two diseases struck together as they did in 1918, the results were especially deadly. But others fell the bacillus was just another opportunistic infection like so many others, and an unseen and unknown viral pneumonia may have been the real killer. At any rate, this combination of diseases could be better dealt with today because we have antibiotics to address the many opportunistic infectious diseases that accompany viral flu and viral pneumonia, even if we can't do anything but provide comfort and care for viral diseases once they have been established. This still leaves the question of why a disproportionate number of young adults died.

One possible answer to this question is the different way humans respond to disease at different stages of life. Sir MacFarlane Burnet, a noted Australian who is one of the century's most known students of influenza and immunology and who won the Nobel Prize for medicine in 1960, suggests that the practice of the body to respond to a new microbe with intense inflammation is the key problem. The process of inflammation brings a quantity of blood, fluid, antibodies, and white blood cells to the area being attacked by the microbe. This process of inflammation is like a nation responding to foreign attack by mobilizing of its troops.

However, in a child, the inflammation process is usually just equal to the attack because the child is still learning how to mobilize against general infection. The child usually will survive, but not always, as the child learns to deal with the normal onslaught of childhood diseases. In children, excess reactions like that of the mucous membranes against relatively harmless bits of pollen are rare. By the time young adulthood is reached, a person has learned to rather routinely handle all the childhood diseases, and the attention of the body is turned to address localized injuries such as broken bones and wounds (this is a process that has developed over centuries). Now the young adult must respond with an intense inflammation process to fix the injury or wound quickly and get back in the hunt. After 40 years of age or so, this ability to produce an intense inflammation process declines.

The result in 1918–19 was that when the flu virus attacked the trachea and the alveoli of the lungs, especially if it were a virus that was very virulent and unrecognized by the body which the pandemic was thought to consist of, the response was so intense that the fluid build-up in the lungs, in the simplest way to state it, drowned the victim. This is why so many soldiers, for example, seemed to fall sick on one day and die on the next as they turned blue and then purple, unable to breathe properly. Autopsies showed their lungs to be full of fluid and no longer light and airy as they should be.

Children continued to produce their "muddle-through" response as best they could. Adults over 40 had their normal less-intense response to local attack, which results in older people being less able to respond to localized injury of any type, even as they maintain their learned life-long response to generalized microbe attacks. The overall result was the W-shaped mortality curves shown in the figure.

There is no proof of this theory, and there is no way to ethically test it. It seems to be vaguely corroborated by the fact that childhood diseases are often more deadly in adults than in children, in the few cases when adults get such diseases. It also appears that the Black Death that ravaged England in the mid-fourteenth century also more readily killed young adults than children and older adults, but data are sketchy. One thing that seems sure is that when a new disease strikes a population that has not seen it before, the results may be quite different than common-wisdom projects.

APPENDIX 8:
DRUGS MOST FREQUENTLY
PRESCRIBED, 2001

Rank	Name of Drug (principal generic substance)	Times prescribed	Therapeutic Use
1.	Lipitor (atorvastatin calcium)	21,223	Lowers cholesterol
2.	Celebrex (celecoxib)	17,608	Anti-inflammatory agent
3.	Vioxx (rofecoxib)	15,265	Anti-inflammatory agent
4.	Claritin (loratadine)	14,640	Antihistamine
5.	Lasix (furosemide)	13,834	Diuretic, antihyptertensive
6.	Synthroid (levothyroxine)	13,667	Thyroid hormone therapy
7.	Premarin (estrogens)	13,023	Estrogen replacement therapy
8.	Tylenol (acetaminophen)	12,626	Analgesic (for pain relief)
9.	Prednisone	12,234	Steroid replacement therapy/ anti-inflammatory agent
10.	Albuterol sulfate	12,044	Antihistamatic/bronchodilator
11.	Prilosec (omeprazole)	11,054	For duodenal or gastric ulcer
12.	A.S.A. (acetylsalicyclic acid, aspirin)	10,875	Analgesic (for pain relief)
13.	Aspirin	10,791	Analgesic (for pain relief)
14.	Zocor (simvastatin)	10,468	Lowers cholesterol
15.	Paxil	10,218	Antidepressant
16.	Atenolol	10,098	For high blood pressure
17.	Amoxicillin	9,940	Antibiotic
18.	Zoloft (sertraline hydrochloride)	9,750	Antidepressant
19.	Norvasc (amlodipine besylate)	9,748	For high blood pressure
20.	Glucophage (metformin)	9,663	Blood glucose regulator
	All other	1,065,016	

The table above shows the drugs most frequently prescribed in the offices of physicians in 2001, the last year for which full data are available. The table shows the name of the drug, the number of times it was prescribed, and the intended therapeutic use of the drug. This list is only an overview of the total therapeutic drug usage in the United States, but it does show trends and it gives a good indication of which problems are commonly treated by therapeutic drugs. Comparing the list, which is compiled by the U.S. Public Health Service, on a year-by-year basis can show which drugs come suddenly into favor and which are prescribed routinely every year. We will look at this type of comparison shortly, but first we need to discuss the overall prescription drug situation in the United States as of 2004, because it has changed substantially during the second half of the twentieth century.

As described in this book, prescribed drugs were not a major cost item when Medicare was established in 1965. Antibiotics were a major part of prescribed drugs then, and antibiotics were, and still are, generally relatively cheap. But in the last 40 years, major advances have been made in the development of drugs, and they now form the first line of defense in the battle against many degenerative diseases. Drugs of all types now are part of any doctor's treatment program, and because such drugs are typically taken every day and are newly developed, meaning they are still under patent protection, the cost of prescription drugs has become a major part of medical costs.

Because drugs now form a significant part of medical costs, the Medicare program announced on June 27, 2003, its intention to offer a prescription drug program, with the program going into effect starting in 2006. Already, in 2004, Medicare recipients can obtain drug cards offering discounts on drugs. However, many complaints have arisen that the discounts are no better than those already obtainable from other sources. Further, many seniors are having their prescriptions filled in Canada, Mexico, and via the Internet to save costs, but in many cases the safety and effectiveness of drugs obtained outside the United States is in question. The proposed Medicare drug plan is quite complex and requires contributions by the users. The issue of the growing costs of drugs will be with us for a long time. But part of the problem is that many newly developed drugs are truly miracle drugs that definitely save or extend lives. At some level, these new dramatic developments have to be paid for.

The table shown in Appendix 8 indicates the source of some of these cost problems. The top 20 drugs represent only a combined total of about 20 percent of all prescriptions written. Even Lipitor, the most prescribed drug, represents only about 1.6 percent of all prescriptions written. Thus, there is an incredible variety of prescribed drugs, and many of them are intended for very specific problems, and this relatively narrow product base drives up the cost. Further, even though Amoxicillin, a relatively cheap antibiotic, still comes in at number 17 on the list (it was number one in 1997 and 1998), and "dirt-cheap" aspirin occupies places number 12 and 13, Lipitor, the top-ranked drug, costs typically at least a dollar a day even with good discounts. And one can take Lipitor forever, whereas antibiotics and aspirin are typically used on an as-required basis. Even persons who take a daily aspirin for blood-clotting protection spend pennies for the drug, not dollars. Many other drugs can cost several dollars each, and they are also meant to be used indefinitely. An elderly person can easily require several drugs a day, and it can quickly come to the point where choices must be made between drugs and food. In the situations where something like AIDS is being combated, drug costs quickly reach thousands of dollars per month. But however tragic such cases are on an individual basis, they represent only a very narrow segment of the population. The majority of the seniors in the country, however, are on multiple drug regimes for ordinary degenerative conditions, and the number of persons affected is large.

The rapidity with which new (and generally expensive) drugs come into vogue is shown by the fact that the top three drugs on the list in Appendix 8 — Lipitor, Celebrex, and Vioxx — were not in the top 20 in 1997. In 1999, Lipitor had moved up to number five and Celebrex to number 10, but Vioxx had not yet made an appearance. In 2001, these three drugs occupied the top three spots pushing Claritin, which had been number one in the two previous years, down to fourth place. Overall, there were about 1.3 billion prescriptions written in 2001, roughly a 15 percent increase since 1997. Thus, the yearly increase in the number of prescriptions written is relatively nominal, reaching a little less than four percent annually.

The 20 most-prescribed drugs address 11 different conditions, with three each being prescribed for high blood pressure and pain relief and two each for high cholesterol, depression, anti-inflammation, and antihistamine uses. Sometimes, drugs intended primarily for one condition can be used to alleviate another. At any rate, there is no one outstanding condition for which most of the top 20 drugs are prescribed. But high blood pressure and high cholesterol are conditions encountered normally in upper middle age, and the five drugs prescribed for these two conditions represent 25 percent of the top 20 drugs.

APPENDIX 9:
FATAL OCCUPATIONAL
INJURIES, 2002

	Fatalities	
	Number	*Percent*
Transportation Incidents	2,381	43
Assaults and Violent Acts	840	15
Contact with Objects and Equipment	873	16
Falls	714	13
Exposure to Harmful Substance or Environments	538	10
Fires and Explosions	165	3
Other Events or Exposures	13	—
Total	5,524	100

The table above shows the number of occupational fatalities in the United States in 2002. It shows both the number of fatalities in each category and the percentage of total fatalities occurring in the category. The percentage of fatalities in each category has remained relatively constant since 1998, but the total number of fatalities fell by about 8 percent between 1998 and 2002.

Many people will be surprised by some of the information contained in the numbers shown in the table in Appendix 9. Whereas the phrase "occupational fatalities" often brings to mind fires and explosions at huge industrial complexes like oil refineries, or miners trapped in mines or workers caught in gigantic machines, by far the greatest number of occupational fatalities are caused by ordinary transportation incidents, with most of these being simple collisions on the nation's highways. In a country where 44,000 people are killed in motor vehicle accidents in a typical year (2002 had exactly that number, and the total changes little from year to year), perhaps it should not be surprising that transportation incidents are the leading cause of death among occupational fatalities. But the total fatalities in this category are only a little over 4 percent of the total number of people killed in the United States on its highways.

In 2002, 43 percent of all occupational fatalities fell into the "Transportation Incidents" category. As noted above, the percentage in this category has barely budged since 1998. It is hard to conceive of any new safety techniques to reduce accidents in this area that have not already been tried on the public as a whole, but in the summer of 2004 there were reports that some companies were planning to ban the use of cell phones by their drivers when driving on the basis that such use was a distraction and thus unsafe.

The next category on the list, which may also be a surprise due to its size, is that of "Assaults and Violent Acts." This category accounted for 15 percent of all fatalities in 2002, just behind the 16 percent accounted for by "Contacts With Objects and Equipment," the second biggest category. Once again, perhaps the size of the assaults category may not be a surprise in a country that seems to suffer from an increasing level of personal violence in many situations. Occupational fatalities in the assaults category have actually decreased slightly since 1998, even though the term "going postal" to describe an enraged person seems to have entered the language due to the unfortunate series of shootings in post office facilities over the past several years. The most logical step to improve safety in this category would appear to be increased security and screening for weapons at industrial facilities, but when one considers the number of workplaces in the United States, this may be an impossible task. Perhaps we are at the place where assaults and violent acts have become truly an occupational hazard.

Another category that should catch our attention is that of "Falls." This is the fourth largest category at 13 percent of all fatalities. One can think of many things to increase safety in this category, but many older persons (not necessarily seniors) suffer from falls every year. It is a common reason for admissions to emergency rooms, and many people can remember instances where they got momentarily dizzy and lost their balance for no apparent reason. The body is a very complex organism, and standing and walking is not a natural act. Every child must learn both from scratch. The best safety device in this case is great individual care in walking. Since a person suffering a fatal fall can not be interviewed to determine what happened, we can never know how many fatal falls were due to unsafe conditions and how many were due to neurological accidents that are not subject to safety precautions.

"Contacts with Objects and Equipment" perhaps contains more of the kinds of events we often think of as occupational accidents. But this category accounted for only one-sixth of all fatalities. Similarly, the category of "Exposure to Harmful Substance or Environments" may seem more compatible with thoughts about occupational accidents, but this category accounted for only 10 percent of all fatalities. Finally, the category of "Fires and Explosions" would seem to be a key occupational worry, but it is the smallest category of all, accounting for only 3 percent of all fatalities.

This means that what we might call the most expected categories of occupational fatalities account only for 29 percent of all fatalities. Also, the total number of fatalities is relatively low at 5,524 per year. Compared to the 44,000 motor vehicle fatalities noted above, this means nearly ten times as many people are killed driving their cars each year than are killed in all possible ways in occupational accidents (and the biggest single occupational killer also happens to be driving a vehicle).

To put occupational fatalities in perspective, there were 33,300 deaths from home accidents in the United States in 2002, almost exactly six times as many fatalities as occurred in an occupational setting. Further, accidents at home do not include any motor vehicle problems or issues associated with large machinery. In the United States in total, there were about 100,000 deaths due to accidents in 2002, with over three-quarters of these coming from motor vehicle accidents (44,000) plus accidents in the home (33,000). Objectively, in spite of all we hear about workplace safety, fatalities in a workplace setting are a very small part of total deaths in the United States. Now if the problem in the workplace were addressed from a standpoint of workplace injuries, lost time, and the costs of health care (including worker's compensation et al), the discussion would take a different turn.

There have been dramatic changes in the kind of accidents that happen in the home over the past five decades. In 2002, there were 33,300 fatalities due to home accidents, with 24 percent due to falls and 38 percent due to poisoning. These two categories were about 62 percent of the total. In 1950, there were 29,000 deaths due to home accidents, not much different than the 2002 total. Also in 1950, about 60 percent of the total was due to falls and poisoning, again not much different from 2002. But where 24 percent died from falls in 2002, the percentage was 51 percent in 1950, more than twice as high. And where only 9 percent died of poisoning in 1950, 38 percent did so in 2002, more than four times as high. The data are somewhat skewed because deaths from falls dropped by about 50 percent between 1950 and 1980 and have remained relatively constant since. Thus, most of the change between 1950 and 2002 had already occurred by 1980. But that does not explain why it happened.

One would need a breakdown of how many such deaths were suffered by elderly persons versus children to get a better understanding of why deaths due to falls decreased so much and poisoning deaths increased so much between 1950 and 2002. But this is consistent with general national accidental death rates even over just the last three decades. Since 1970, death rates due to falls have decreased as they leveled off in the 1980s, while death rates due to poisoning have generally continually increased, doubling just in the time between 1970 and the beginning of this century. One could assume that medicine cabinets are now much fuller of medicines that can turn into poison than they used to be, but the question of why they are apparently more accessible to children is not clear. At any rate, if home poisonings were eliminated, over 12,000 lives could be saved annually. This is more than twice the number of deaths due to occupational accidents of all types, including those due to occupational motor vehicle accidents. As always, accidental deaths need to be put into proper perspective to decide where resources should be placed to try to avoid them.

APPENDIX 10:
AIDS DEATHS AND
NEW CASES, 1985–2002

Year	AIDS Deaths	AIDS New Cases
1985	6,854	8,161
1990	31,988	41,448
1993	44,108	102,082
1994	48,110	77,092
1995	52,254	70,412
1999	18,484	44,580
2000	17,347	40,290
2001	17,402	41,450
2002	16,371	42,475

The table above shows the number of new cases of AIDS and the number of deaths caused by AIDS in the United States between 1985 and 2002. Some of the values may not agree with all sources, because the definition of AIDS cases has changed for reporting purposes as more has been learned about AIDS. Thus, some reported numbers have increased over time.

As the table shows, the number of new cases of AIDS peaked just above 100,000 in 1993. The number of deaths from AIDS peaked just above 50,000 in 1995. The advent of drugs that delay the development of HIV infection into a full-blown case of AIDS and the development of drugs that increase the life span of those who already have AIDS have combined to reduce both the number of new cases and the number of deaths. Further, educational measures about how HIV and AIDS are spread and what to do to prevent their spread have also contributed to greatly reducing the number of people who become HIV positive and eventually develop AIDS.

The number of new cases of AIDS has fallen by 40 percent since 1995 and by almost 60 percent since the peak in 1993. The number of deaths has fallen by almost 70 percent since 1995 and also by 70 percent since the peak near 1995. In 2002, the number of new cases was 42,475, and the number of deaths was 16,371. AIDS no longer appears on the top ten leading causes of death in the United States and accounted for less than 0.7 percent of all deaths in 2002. The percentage of deaths caused by AIDS is much higher in the 25–44 age group (especially among men), but even in that age range accidents are usually the biggest killer.

Since 1985, males have accounted for over 80 percent of all new AIDS cases. Even today, they typically account for 75 percent of all new cases. Since 1985, 57 percent of all new AIDS cases occurred in the category of men having sex with men; 21 percent occurred among intravenous drug users; and almost 8 percent occurred among men in both categories. Thus, since 1985, almost 86 percent of all new AIDS cases occurred among men having sex with men and/or using intravenous drugs. Even today, these categories account for about 70 percent of all new AIDS cases. In women, who now account for only about 25 percent of all new cases, the overwhelming number of new cases of AIDS come from those who are intravenous drug users, those who have sex with intravenous drug users, and those who have unprotected sex with men.

Thus, educational material targeting these groups (promoting the use of condoms in any sexual encounter and avoiding intravenous drugs and/or the sharing of needles) has helped to reduce the incidence of new cases of AIDS. Because AIDS is a difficult disease to get (it requires the interchange of bodily fluids), educational material can help greatly in its prevention. In the United States, AIDS is considered by public health officials to be basically under control but much vigilance is needed to keep it that way. It is still an incurable disease without any available vaccine, even if new drugs are helping to extend life spans for those who contract it.

In the world outside the United States, AIDS is far from being under control. In 2003, new AIDS cases worldwide are estimated to have numbered 5 million — the most ever. In Africa alone, AIDS deaths were estimated to be more than 3 million. The basic causes of AIDS are the same everywhere — unsafe sex and intravenous drug use with dirty needles — but prevention programs vary widely in effectively due to limited resources, fear and ignorance, and corrupt political leaders.

As described in this book, the virus causing AIDS is believed to have originated in the jungles and rain forests of Africa and crossed over from monkeys to humans. AIDS is believed to have originated in the Belgian Congo sometime between the late 1940s and early 1950s. Its first victim was identified in 1959. But in 1967 a much more lethal virus called the Marburg virus emerged from the jungles. In 1976 an even more lethal virus called the Ebola virus was found. One form of Ebola is estimated to kill 90 percent of the people who contact it, and death comes in days, not in years, as in the case of the AIDS virus.

More viruses of these types are expected to be encountered as mankind goes deeper into the jungles and rain forests of the world. Viruses appear to have been on earth much longer than mankind, and they may become mankind's ultimate contender for primacy on earth. In this sense, keeping even the AIDS virus under control in the United States may become the ultimate task of public health and medicine.

BIBLIOGRAPHY

The bibliography shows the key books consulted in putting together this chronology. Probably the most comprehensive book in this list is *Magic Shots* by Alan Chase. This book may be technically challenging for some people, but it is essentially a history of the development of various vaccines and drugs used in the battle against infectious diseases. However the book also includes many minibiographies of the key scientists who developed the various drugs and a brief history of their work. Another reasonably inclusive book is *The Sanitarians* by John Duffy. This is an overview of the sanitarian movement and how it contributed to the development of public health in the United States.

A book that covers a more specific subject is *America's Forgotten Pandemic* by Alfred Crosby. This is a well-detailed book about the flu epidemic of 1918–1919. It includes considerable detail about both the epidemic and an analysis of why the epidemic was so deadly.

Another excellent book about a specific subject is *Doctor Jenner and the Speckled Monster* by Alberti Marrin. This book covers not only the pioneering work done by Dr. Jenner in the eighteenth century but also serves as a history of how smallpox impacted the world in early times and how it was eradicated, except for the stores currently kept by various countries.

A definitive history of the development of the Salk polio vaccine is the subject of *Patenting the Sun* by Jane Smith. This book not only contains an almost daily history of the events of the early 1950s that led up to testing of the Salk polio vaccine, but it also contains an excellent history of the development of the March of Dimes, which in turn made the development of the Salk polio vaccine possible.

A final book that covers essentially one subject within the broad range of public health history is *The Hot Zone* by Richard Preston. This book describes in detail the outbreaks in Africa of the Marburg and Ebola viruses that are presently the most deadly viruses known of those that have emerged from the jungles and rain forests of Africa. Few people know that the Ebola virus once paid a visit to the United States. This book traces the history of that event as well as the emergence of the viruses in Africa and the attempts made by the Centers for Disease Control in the United States to track and defend against the viruses.

Aaron, Henry J. *Serious and Unstable Condition: Financing America's Health Care.* Washington, D.C.: The Brookings Institution, 1991.

Bridgewater, William, and Seymour Kurtz, eds. *The Columbia Encyclopedia.* 3rd ed. New York: Columbia University Press, 1963.

Chase, Allan. *Magic Shots: A Human and Scientific Account of the Long and Continuing Struggle to Eradicate Infectious Diseases by Vaccination.* New York: William Morrow and Company, 1982.

Crosby, Alfred W. *America's Forgotten Pandemic: The Influenza of 1918.* New York: Cambridge University Press, 2003.

Duffy, John. *The Sanitarians: A History of American Public Health.* Chicago: University of Illinois Press, 1990.

Garrett, Laurie. *The Coming Plague: Newly Emerging Diseases in a World Out of Balance.* New York: Penguin Books, 1994.

Grob, Gerald. *The Deadly Truth: A History of Disease in America.* Cambridge, Mass.: Harvard University Press, 2002.

Hargrove, Jim. *The Story of Jonas Salk and the Discovery of the Polio Vaccine.* Chicago: Children's Press, 1990.

Kraut, Alan M. *Silent Travelers: Germs, Genes, and the "Immigrant Menace."* New York: HarperCollins, 1994.

Law, Sylvia A. *Blue Cross: What Went Wrong?* New Haven, Conn.: Yale University Press, 1976.

Marrin, Alberi. *Dr. Jenner and the Speckled Monster: The Search for the Smallpox Vaccine.* New York: Dutton Children's Books, 2002.

McGeveran, William A. Jr., ed. *The World Almanac and Book of Facts, 2004.* New York: World Almanac Books, 2004.

McNeill, William H. *Plagues and Peoples.* New York: Anchor Books/Doubleday, 1977.

Ott, Katherine. *Fevered Lives: Tuberculosis in American Culture since 1870.* Cambridge, Mass.: Harvard University Press, 1996.

Porter, Dorothy. *Health, Civilization and the State: A History of Public Health from Ancient to Modern Times.* New York: Routledge, 1999.

Preston, Richard. *The Hot Zone.* New York: Anchor Books/Doubleday, 1994.

Rosen, George. *A History of Public Health.* Baltimore: The Johns Hopkins University Press, 1993.

Smith, Jane S. *Patenting the Sun: Polio and the Salk Vaccine.* New York: Anchor Books/Doubleday, 1990.

Starr, Paul. *The Social Transformation of American Medicine.* New York: Basic Books, 1982.

Tiner, John Hudson. *100 Scientists Who Shaped World History.* San Mateo, Calif.: Bluewood Books, 2000.

Vance Dorey, Annette K. *Better Baby Contests: The Scientific Quest for Perfect Child-hood Health in the Early Twentieth Century*. Jefferson, N.C.: McFarland & Company, 1999.

Wright, Russell O. *Life and Death in the United States*. Jefferson, N.C.: McFarland & Company, 1997.

Yenne, Bill, and Dr. Morton Grossner. *100 Inventions That Shaped World History*. San Mateo, Calif.: Bluewood Books, 1993.

INDEX